Errata

Page 122

The last two sentences of the paragraph unde... the heading 'Grants' should read as follows:

For example, a single Honours chemistry degree student will receive about 2000 Euros for a full academic year. However, a chemistry and German combined degree student, for whom the study of German is a necessary part of the course, would only receive approximately 600 Euros.

Page 204

The first item in the list under the heading 'ISP charges' should read as follows:

The cost of calls to the helpline – while with most providers, these are local or national call rated, for the Dixons helpline calls are charged at the premium rate of 50p a minute, but there is extensive on-line help and a free e-mail help service;

Page 184

Fig A.1 should contain the pointers shown here:

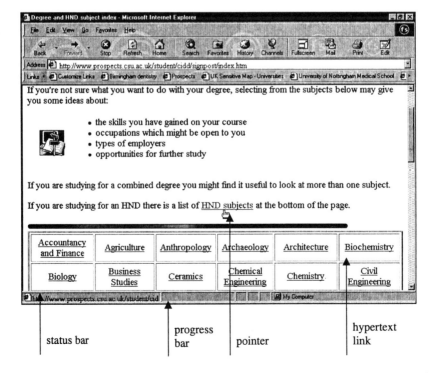

NET THAT COURSE!

NET THAT COURSE!

Using the Internet to research, select and apply for degree courses

Irene Krechowiecka

KOGAN
PAGE

YOURS TO HAVE AND TO HOLD
BUT NOT TO COPY

First published in 1999

Apart from any fair dealing for the purposes of research or private study, or criticism or review, as permitted under the Copyright, Designs and Patents Act 1988, this publication may only be reproduced, stored or transmitted, in any form or by any means, with the prior permission in writing of the publishers, or in the case of reprographic reproduction in accordance with the terms and licences issued by the CLA. Enquiries concerning reproduction outside these terms should be sent to the publishers at the undermentioned address:

Kogan Page Limited
120 Pentonville Road
London N1 9JN

© Irene Krechowiecka, 1999

The right of Irene Krechowiecka to be identified as the author of this work has been asserted by her in accordance with the Copyright, Designs and Patents Act 1988.

British Library Cataloguing in Publication Data

A CIP record for this book is available from the British Library.

ISBN 0 7494 2958 5

Typeset by Jean Cussons Typesetting, Diss, Norfolk
Printed and bound in Great Britain by Biddles Ltd, Guildford and King's Lynn

Contents

Contents

Contents

Preface

Every care has been taken to check the currency and accuracy of information, but inevitably things will change. The material contained in this book is set out in good faith for general guidance and no liability can be accepted for loss or expense incurred as a result of relying in particular circumstances on statements made in the book. Laws and regulations are complicated and subject to change and readers should check the current position with the relevant authorities before making personal arrangements. Suggestions for alterations and additions are welcome and can be sent to:

irene.k@unforgettable.com

All screen shots are the copyright of their authors. All product names and/or logos are trademarks of their respective owners. Their inclusion in this book does not imply their owners' endorsement of it.

Acknowledgements

I would like to thank everyone who took the time to talk and write to me about their use of the Internet. I'm especially grateful to all those Web designers whose pages made this book a pleasure to research. Particular thanks to Chris for all the saxophone accompaniment and Rob for masterful use of the red pen.

Introduction

Hard questions must have hard answers.

Plutarch

Over the last few years, the only thing that has been constant is change. 'New' must be one of the most exhausted words in the language. If you are now in the position of researching higher education you are bombarded with information on new courses, new funding arrangements, the dilemma of a new versus an old university, new European and international opportunities ... the list goes on and on.

One of the effects of these changes has been increased scrutiny of the value of degrees. Students, their families, employers and the media are asking questions about, and contributing to, the debate on the future of higher education. In a changing world, answers change regularly, but in relation to higher education choices, the questions largely remain the same. This book draws your attention to the questions you should be asking yourself and others before you can make an informed decision about what you should study and where. It highlights the full range of opportunities, giving the basic information you need for an overview of the situation and directing you to sources of detailed information that will keep you updated. Those sources are all on the Internet – the newest of communication technologies.

This beguiling medium has the potential to add to the information overload many of us are suffering from. *Net That*

Course! pinpoints the resources that provide valuable information and shows how to use them effectively. There are so many worthwhile Internet resources in relation to higher education that it's been a challenge to keep the number of sites suggested down. Those listed are ones that provide quality information from official and informal sources, to help you get a rounded picture of what's available.

To fit in the necessary research for making choices about the next stage of your life alongside all your study, you need to be focused and organized in your approach. This book encourages you to work through your options methodically, to review and document progress. The chapters have checklists to help you keep track of what you've done and what you need to do. In this age of all things new and wonderful, the old paper and pencil still have a use!

1
Questions and Choices

Students and their families are asking searching questions about the value of degrees, and looking for hard, objective information to help with choices that will have financial, vocational and social implications for the rest of their lives. The Internet can help you provide the answers.

- A changing world
- Where do you start?
- Good reasons for going to university
- Less good reasons
- What's the Internet got to do with all this?
- Internet safety
- Evaluating material
- All the other questions
- Sites worth seeing

A CHANGING WORLD

You've decided that study at a higher level is a worthwhile investment in your future. Now you have the deceptively simple-sounding task of finding up to six courses to apply for. What you are faced with is an exciting but potentially bewildering array of options and possibilities.

Recent developments in higher education include:

- the replacement of grants by loans;
- the introduction of tuition fees;
- greater scrutiny of the vocational value of degrees;
- league tables and comparisons of higher education institutions;
- a growing interest in industrial sponsorship;
- stronger links between industry and degree courses;
- increased European and international links;
- a wider range of courses;
- flexible approaches to time and place of study, subject combination and assessment methods.

Changes over the last decade have resulted in almost a third of under-21-year-olds undertaking a higher education course. There are plans to expand this to 45 per cent. Expansions in higher education have not always been matched by expansions in the graduate labour market, and this a major concern for those considering university. The aim of this book is to show you how Internet-based information can help with researching options and their implications quickly and effectively, so that choices are informed and realistic.

The main questions to answer are the following.

- Why is university right for me?
- What subject(s) do I want to study?
- What am I capable of academically?
- Which are the best courses for my needs?
- What makes a 'good' degree course?
- Where would I like to live while I study?
- What will my course lead to after graduation?
- How much is it going to cost and how am I going to pay for it?
- What work experience and international opportunities will it give me?
- How and when do I apply?
- Do I need a break from education?

Each of these 'big' questions gives rise to many smaller ones. It's easy to feel overwhelmed by the research needed to make the best choice. All this at a time when you're under pressure to study hard to secure a place at university. It can be made manageable if you take a methodical approach and have access to accurate, comprehensive, impartial and up-to-date information.

WHERE DO YOU START?

The very first question to have to ask yourself is 'Why is university right for me?' Going to university represents a substantial investment in yourself. It's essential that you are clear about what you expect from a university education. Only then can you check that the courses you apply for meet your expectations.

A survey by *The Times* of sixth-formers applying to university in 1998 found that 67 per cent were applying because they felt a degree would give them a career advantage, 29 per cent had a strong interest in the subject to be studied and the rest were going for social reasons. The best starting point is a list of your own reasons for wanting to go to university. This can later form the basis of your application.

GOOD REASONS FOR GOING TO UNIVERSITY

If you are not sure why you want to go to university here are some possibilities to choose from.

'Having a degree will give me more career choices.'

This has been the case and there is every reason to believe it will continue to be. The Association of Graduate Recruiters (AGR) is forecasting a continuing increase in graduate vacancies. You can look at such vacancies on the Web and check the latest information on graduate recruitment trends through the AGR site. Use employers' Web sites and see what they are actually doing now in terms of graduate recruitment. Many – such as Unilever, Shell, KPMG and British Telecom – make positive, encouraging statements about their attitude to graduates (see Chapters 4 and 5).

'I will be able to get better-paid work as a graduate.'

By their early thirties, male graduates earn 12 to 18 per cent and females 34 to 38 per cent more, on average, than those who went into work with at least one A level (reported in *What do Graduates Do?*, AGCAS, 1999).

Table 1.1 Forecast graduate starting salaries for 1998

	(£)	% Change 1997–98
Top 10%	20,000	5.1
Top 25%	17,600	3.5
Median	16,000	3.2
Bottom 25%	15,000	2.2
Bottom 10%	14,580	4.1

Source: Graduate Salaries and Vacancies Survey, 1998, Institute for Employment Studies for The Association of Graduate Recruiters

However, it is no longer possible to generalize about graduate jobs. They range from management training schemes to work in fast food outlets. To research graduate employment, see Chapters 2 and 3.

'I need a degree for my chosen career.'

Many professions have degree only entry. Some, such as medicine or physiotherapy, require a particular course; others, such as law or teaching, have entry routes for graduates from a range of disciplines. The Web sites of professional bodies and organizations specializing in careers advice for graduates give comprehensive, up-to-date information on entry requirements. To check that the degree you choose does fulfil the entry criteria of the profession you are aiming for, see Chapter 2.

'I enjoy studying and I'm good at it.'

If this is not the case, then you shouldn't be considering higher education! To benefit from university you have to be enthusiastic about your subject, able to cope with study at a higher level and gain pleasure from it. You may choose to continue with a subject you've enjoyed at school, take up a new area of study or combine new with old. Whatever subject you choose, you will find a wealth of material on the Internet that enables you to see what in-depth study of that discipline involves. You'll be able to dip into research, publications and discussions on every specialism in every subject offered. To do this, see Chapters 2 and 3.

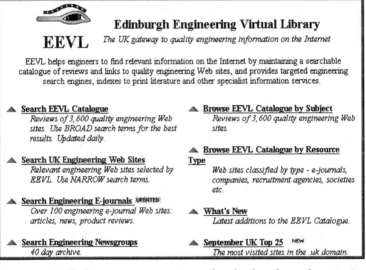

Figure 1.1 Subject gateway sites take the hard work out of finding relevant material on the Internet

'It's an opportunity and experience I don't want to miss.'

Going to university gives you the chance to explore new ideas and activities, meet new people, live independently, travel, study and work abroad. Use this book and the Web to explore just what is on offer.

'I'm not ready to make a career decision yet.'

Doing a degree can keep your career options open. Many employers recruit graduates with a degree in any subject. Forty per cent of graduates go into jobs not related to their university studies. However, if you have no idea of what you want to do, you could choose the wrong course. Explore what different subjects can lead to in terms of employment (see Figures 2.2 and A.1) and do a self-assessment exercise that will help you focus on a range of options (see Figure 2.1).

LESS GOOD REASONS

It's easy to be carried along by what everyone else is doing and make choices for reasons that do not stand up to close scrutiny.

'If I don't go to university its a waste of my sixth-form studies.'

Not true. There are many opportunities for school-leavers with A levels or Advanced GNVQs that offer excellent training. Examples include retail management, journalism and accountancy. Such schemes generally require 20+ A level points or a distinction in the appropriate GNVQ.

'I can't think of anything else to do and I want to get away from home.'

Consider taking some time out. If you've no real enthusiasm for a particular subject, vocational area or study for its own sake, going to university could be an expensive waste of time. Taking time off from study gives you the chance to experience something different, move away from home, earn and save money, try out a job or range of jobs. It provides a break from study and the luxury of time to work out what you really want to do.

WHAT'S THE INTERNET GOT TO DO WITH ALL THIS?

To make choices effectively, you have to gather and evaluate a lot of information. The Internet is an unsurpassable tool for this. Higher education has been using it as a resource for teaching, research and sharing information for a considerable time. Much of this is publicly available and you can use it to research a credible and impressive application. The advantages of Internet-based information are:

- it's available 24 hours a day, 7 days a week;
- search facilities help you quickly find relevant information;
- the opportunity to look at the same issues from different perspectives — such as the university, employers, professional bodies;
- access to experts in all subject areas – you can eavesdrop on, and participate in, academic discussions;
- the chance to investigate the research interests and publications of university staff.

INTERNET SAFETY

Information on the Internet comes from both individuals and organizations. There is no control and little censorship. As more young people have access to the Internet, concerns about their safety grow. If you are using the Internet at school or college, potentially unsuitable material will be filtered out. For home use, there is a range of software that allows control of Internet use. The most basic is within the browser software itself (see Figure 1.2).

Your service provider will be able to advise you on additional controls and safeguards. More sophisticated filtering software is available from sites listed at the end of this chapter. These are maintained by organizations working to make the Internet a safe and positive experience for all.

Wherever you are accessing the Internet, you have to be aware of the possible dangers. The main issues are:

- personal safety;
- financial security;
- offensive material.

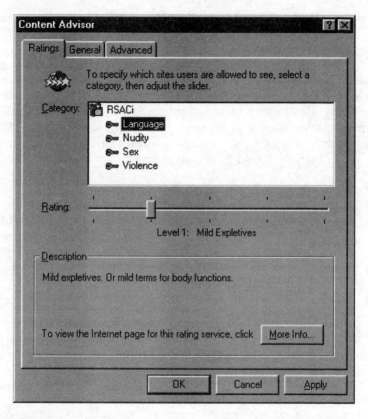

Figure 1.2 Internet Explorer's Content Advisor can provide some filtering

Personal safety

The Internet is both personal and anonymous. People can hide or protect their identity behind an e-mail address or a chat line name, and so can you. There is no problem until you start to divulge personal details. Take the usual precautions you would when dealing with any stranger. Because you can't see or hear the person it's all too easy for someone to pretend to be something they're not. The handsome hunk or gorgeous girl you thought you'd been chatting to could be a spotty 14-year-old or a dirty old man! There are guidelines designed to protect you (see Figure 1.11). The basic rules of Internet safety are:

- never give out personal information, such as your address or phone number, to a stranger;
- tell a teacher or your parents if you come across anything that makes you feel uncomfortable;
- never arrange to get together with someone you have 'met' online without checking with your parents – such meetings should always be in a public place and you should have an adult with you.

Financial security

There is little you need to spend money on in the context of researching a degree course. However, if you to buy a book, pay to go on a course or book a ticket to travel to an interview, you'll be able to do it online. Although there are worries about the security of financial transactions on the Web, it is generally accepted that credit card purchases on secure sites (see Figure 1.3) are as safe as giving your details over the phone. Browsers such as Explorer and Navigator use SSL (Secure Sockets Layer), which encrypts the data you send so that no one can read or change it during transmission. This doesn't remove all the risks, however. You are trusting the server administrator with your credit card number and no technology can protect you from dishonest or careless people. One great advantage of paying this way is that if you do not get the services or goods you paid for, you may be reimbursed. *This does not apply to transactions using debit cards such us Switch.*

Offensive material

Internet content reflects all that is good and bad in the world. The good far outweighs the bad, but its possible to stumble across things that are offensive. You are in control of what you look at and can always close a Web page down.

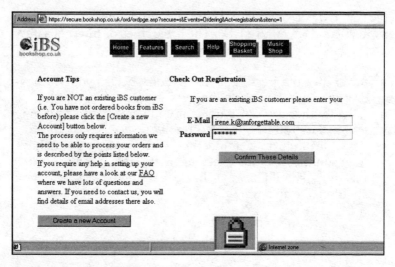

Figure 1.3 A secure site has a closed padlock in the status bar and its address starts with https (see Appendix)

EVALUATING MATERIAL

The Internet is a great free for all and, consequently, the quality of information varies enormously. New technologies mean that finding information is easier than ever before. The abilities needed today are evaluating material and preventing yourself being overloaded. All the sites in this book are examples of good-quality information and the number has been pared to a minimum.

Check where the information comes from, and look at it critically. You need to have access to comprehensive, up-to-date and accurate information. Ideally it should be objective too, but very little ever is. Every individual and organization has a point of view they wish to promote. Specific points to check are:

● when it was last updated;
● the author and their purpose.

Information from universities, learned societies, academic journals, careers advisory centres, government departments

```
780 Music

    780 Music: general resources              Music subject terms:
    780 Music: departments and institutions
    780 Music: education and research         | jazz music              ▼ |
    780 Music: journals and magazines          | Search |   | Reset |
    780 Music: libraries
    780.285 Music software                     |   Music resources in the UK   |
    780.82 Women in music
    780.89 Ethnomusicology                     |    All music resources A-Z    |
    780.9 Music of specific areas
    780.9 Music of specific periods
    780.92 Composers
    781 General principles and traditions of music
    782 Vocal music
    782.1 Opera
    784 Orchestral and instrumental ensembles and their music
    784.19 Musical instruments: general resources
    785 Chamber music
    786 Keyboard and percussion instruments
    787 Stringed instruments
    788 Wind instruments
    788.9 Brass instruments
```

Figure 1.4   Academic compilations like BUBL's catalogue of Internet resources are of good quality sites

and professional bodies is usually of a high standard (see Figure 1.4), but it should not be regarded as objective. They are each promoting themselves and their point of view. That is why visits to universities, work experience, taster courses and other opportunities to see for yourself are essential too.

ALL THE OTHER QUESTIONS

When you've established the main reasons for wanting to go to university you can start to think about the 'smaller' ones.

'What's the quickest way of getting a short list of suitable courses?'

Once you know what you want to study, you can use books, computer programs or Internet search facilities to produce a list of courses. Computer-based searches allow you to enter

My selected courses ... 127 sport degree courses in the North West
Print this list or click on individual courses for entry requirements

	Course Level	Course Code	Course Length
Liverpool John Moores Univ			
Sports Science	BSc	B600	3FT
Applied Psychology and Sports Science	Mod	CB86	3FT
Manchester Metropolitan Univ			
Sport, Coaching and Exercise Science	BSc	B600	3FT
Health Studies/Sport	Mod	BB69	3FT
Life Science/Sport	Mod	BC61	3FT
Environmental Science/Sport	Mod	BF69	3FT
Applied Social Studies/Sport	Mod	BL63	3FT
Leisure Studies/Sport	Mod	BL64	3FT
Sport/Psychology	Mod	BL67	3FT
Geography/Sport	Mod	BL68	3FT
Cultural Studies/Sport	Mod	BL67	3FT
Sport/Sociology	Mod	BL6J	3FT
Business/Sport	Mod	BN61	3FT

Figure 1.5 The UCAS web site offers an effective way to search for courses. See Chapter 2

criteria that will produce manageable short lists. UCAS has an excellent search facility on its Web site that allows you to produce short lists from the most up-to-date information available (see Figure 1.5 and Chapter 2). Books and computer programs that list, describe and compare courses are widely available in schools and careers centres.

'How can I know if a course is going to suit me until I do it?'

Most courses give you the opportunity to visit or experience a 'taster' session. Departmental Web sites can give you the opportunity to look at lecture notes, essay titles, past exam papers, students projects, recommended reading, even staff biographies (see Figures 2.3, 3.9 and 3.11).

'I left school 15 years ago, is it realistic to think of going back to study?'

Yes, mature students are welcomed by most universities. You'll find information to encourage you on their Web sites (see Figure 1.6). You will need to provide evidence of recent study to support your application in most cases. Investigate Access courses. The UCAS Web site (see Chapter 2) has a database of these one-year courses that are accepted for entry to a degree. You can use them to refresh your study skills or to gain a qualification if you left school without any.

'Is it fair to judge a university department by its Web site?'

No, although it is bound to contribute to your overall impression. Universities use their Web sites as additional marketing tools and marketing material is always flattering. Use the Web site for initial research, but check out the reality for yourself.

'What if I fail all my A levels?'

Some universities offer places on Foundation or Year Zero courses to students with failed or unsuitable A levels and you will find a handful of these vacancies during clearing (see Chapter 7). However, if you fail – rather than just get disappointing grades – you should seriously reassess your aims. You need to be realistic about why this has happened. If you are not suited to academic study, then going to university will simply add to your problems. Speaking to a careers adviser will help you formulate strategies for the future, and you can use the Internet to explore options (see Figure 1.7).

'Is it true that old universities are better than new ones?'

In the published league tables, the older universities consistently come out at the top (see Table 1.2). This creates a popular belief that the older universities are 'better', but you need to look in detail at what that means. All universities have

OLDER STUDENTS

Going to university later in life offers the prospect of even greater challenges than for the student applying from school or college. You would need to consider very carefully how you would adapt not only to new patterns of work, but also to major changes in your lifestyle. You will need to think carefully about your financial, social and family commitments before starting a course – though, of course, the advantages of a degree ultimately outweigh any temporary difficulties.

WOULD YOU FIT IN?

Traditionally LSE has had a higher proportion of 'mature' students (ie, aged 21 or older) than many other universities. We welcome their maturity and the varied experience they have had before coming to university; and we wish to maintain our varied mix of students. LSE also has a large proportion of postgraduate students. This means that the student population at LSE is rather older on average than many other universities, so the older undergraduate should not feel out of place.

WHAT KIND OF CAREER COULD YOU GO INTO?

The section Who chooses LSE? outlines the wide range of careers our graduates go into, and the section. After LSE describes the help offered by our Careers Service. We find that employers welcome LSE graduates in any subject, whether or not it is directly related to a profession; the additional experience and maturity of older graduates can give them an extra advantage in the labour market. Our Careers Service advises students from all backgrounds and at all stages of their studies at LSE – and beyond.

WHAT QUALIFICATIONS WOULD YOU NEED?

We are looking for evidence of recent study and both the ability and the motivation to study at a fairly demanding level. Some mature students will have done O-levels or GCSE, and A/AS-levels, either at school or after a break from study. Others will have various technical or vocational qualfications, or Open University credits. Some, without traditional qualifications, will have taken an Access or Return to Study course. In considering an application based on such a course, we will need to look at the number of contact hours a week between teachers and students, how much written work the course requires of students, and whether the course ends in a formal written examination. Unless you have recently taken a course which was formally examined, we would normally not make an offer of admission without asking you to take our entrance examination and come to an interview. If you have had a break from study after taking a course which was formally examined, we would not normally make an offer of admission without interviewing you. But don't feel too daunted: we will consider your application on its own merits.

Figure 1.6 The London School of Economics has clear guidance for mature students

Figure 1.7 BBC's Student Choice prepares you for the worst! (See Chapter 7)

different strengths and weaknesses. You have to decide what is important to you (employment, cost of accommodation, male/female ratios, relationship with employers, geographical location or setting …). It's more relevant to look at what a university is doing now, how it is regarded by employers and how it meets your needs, than what it did in the past. Use one of the league tables available on the Web to look at how particular institutions meet your criteria. Checklist 3 in Chapter 3 will help you decide on priorities. Information on comparative assessments is given in Chapter 4.

'Will I be in debt forever if I go to university?'

Not quite forever, but potentially for a substantial time after you graduate! The theory is that a graduate's lifetime earnings will be higher than a non-graduate's, so your debt will be repaid and the investment will have been worth while. Predictions about investments of any sort are uncertain. The less debt you get into while at university the better. There are numerous Internet-based resources that can help you explore ways of keeping solvent (see Chapter 5).

Table 1.2 It is easy to see why there's a popular misconception that many of the older universities are 'better' than most of the new ones (See Chapter 4)

Top ten new universities 1998

1998	1997	Overall place 1998	Overall place 1997	
1	1	52	56	Oxford Brookes
2	5	57	59	Sheffield Hallam
3	3	58	58	Robert Gordon
4	4	59	60	West of England
5	2	60	57	Northumbria
6	10	61	65	Brighton
7=	19	62	73	De Montfort
7=	6	63	61	Portsmouth
9	18	64	72	Napier
10	11	65	65	Coventry

Source: The Times' Good University Guide, 1998

'I'm 27, will I feel out of place with all those school-leavers?'

Depending on your choice of course, you may be the youngest in the class. Of the 300,000 people who went on to higher education in 1998, nearly 69,000 were mature students and half of these were over 25. You can find national statistics on the UCAS site and specific details on university or departmental sites.

'How do I find out how employers rate a course?'

Employers may have a preference for graduates from certain courses or universities. You can often find details of these employer links on the careers service or departmental pages of university Web sites. Employers who sponsor students sometimes state a preference for a particular course. See Chapters 3, 4 and 5.

'Is it cheaper to study for a degree in another country?'

With the introduction of fees for UK students, it can at first appear that study in another country is cheaper. However, there are many other factors to be taken into consideration and these are fully explored in Chapter 5. Researching what overseas universities offer is made simple by the Web – every university in the world has a Web site (see Figure 1.8).

BRAINTRACK
University-Index

ASIA FAR EAST CHINA *GUANGDONG*

- Foshan University - Foshan University
- Guangdong University - Guangdong University, Guangzhou
- Guangdong University of Foreign Study - Guangdong University of Foreign Study
- Guangzhou Normal University - Guangzhou Normal University
- Guangzhou University - Guangzhou University, Guangzhou
- Huizhou University - Huizhou University
- Jinan University - Jinan University
- Shantou University - Shantou University, Shantou
- Shenzen University - Shenzen University
- South China Agricultural University - South China Agricultural University
- South China Normal University - South China Normal University
- Sun Yat-Sen University of Medical Science - Sun Yat-Sen University of Medical Science, Guangzhou
- Wuyi University - Wuyi University
- Zhonshan University - Zhonshan Sun Yat-sen University, Guangzhou
- POLYTECHNICS

Home | Search | Alphabetical Country-List

Figure 1.8   You can link to the web sites of most universities in the world from Braintrack's site

'If a course has very low entry requirements, does that mean it's not very good?'

Course entry requirements are not a reflection of quality or academic rigour, but of popularity. You cannot judge a course by the grades asked for – it is much better to look at an independent assessment of it (see Chapter 4). Before investigating courses, you should have a realistic idea of the grades your tutors are predicting for you. These will appear on your reference and are one of the first things admissions tutors look at (see Chapter 7).

'I want to come to Britain to study. Can this book help me?'

You need to do the same research about yourself and your options as UK students. This book will guide you through the process. Some of the financial information in Chapter 5 will not apply to you, but Chapter 8 has detailed information specifically for overseas students. Study is a global activity and international students a feature of most universities across the world. Around 30,000 overseas students enter UK undergraduate courses each year. University Web sites reflect the importance of overseas students, with special sections devoted to their information needs. In some cases they even make linguistic concessions (see Figure 1.9).

Graduiertenstudium in England an der Universität Birmingham

Paßt diese Beschreibung auf Sie?

Welche Vorteile bietet das Graduiertenstudium an der Universität Birmingham?

Was für eine Universität ist Birmingham?

Wie wird die Qualität der Forschung in Großbritannien evaluiert?

Was für eine Stadt ist Birmingham?

Was sind die Vorsaussetzungen des Graduiertenstudiums an der Universität Birmingham?

Der Kostenpunkt

Wo finde ich weitere Informationen?

Sonstige Studienmöglichkeiten in Birmingham

Figure 1.9   English is not the only language on the Web!

'Are Scottish degrees easier or harder?'

There is a misconception that Scottish degrees must be easier because they allow English students with good A levels direct entry to the second year. Academically, there is a similar variation in standards and demands made on students as in England and Wales. Professions such as law and teaching have different entry requirements if you want to work in Scotland. Researching Scottish universities is covered in Chapter 3.

'I'm dyslexic, is university a realistic choice?'

Universities encourage applicants with special needs (see Figure 1.10). If you have the academic potential to succeed, disability of any kind should not be a barrier. Everything in

---

Information Handbook for Disabled Students
City University, Northampton Square, London EC1V 0HB
Foreword
Introduction
Admissions Procedure for Disabled Students
Disability Officer
Student Services and Facilities
- Accommodation
- Library
- Students' Union
- Counselling and Advisory Service
- Careers Services
- Computing Services
- Audio Visual Aids
- Department of Continuing Education
- Rehabilitation Resource Centre

Physical Access
Circulation Map of the Northampton Square Site
Building Details
Financial Support for Students
Safety Matters
Student Profiles
Policy for Promoting Opportunities for People with Disabilities at City University
Code of Practice

This handbook is available in print, large print, on audio tape or computer disk. Tactile versions of the maps are also available.

The text can also be accessed using the World Wide Web at URL http://222.city.ac.uk/city/disabled/handbook.html

---

Figure 1.10 All universities have a section dedicated to students with special needs

this book applies to students with and without special needs. Information specifically for students with a disability is highlighted in the section entitled 'Special concerns' in each chapter. Information on customizing your computer to compensate for disabilities is to be found in the Appendix.

'Why do some courses suggest you only use five of your six UCAS choices for their subject?'

Because they are popular, competition for places is fierce and you need a safety net. This applies to medicine, dentistry and physiotherapy, but can be a good idea for other popular courses (see Chapter 7). It's important that you want to do whatever that sixth choice is. Normally it will be related to the area of your first choice. You need to ask yourself, 'If I end up studying this and working at it for a substantial part of my life, will I always think it's second best?'

'Do universities prefer you to take a year off or keep up non-stop studying?'

In most cases, course tutors are happy for students to take a year off before starting their course. In areas such as maths, tutors may worry that a break from studying the subject could impair your ability. It's always a good idea to check an individual department's attitude to taking time off. They may have a statement about it on their Web site or an e-mail address for tutors (see Chapter 3). You may have a greater problem convincing your parents that it's a good idea. They might worry that you'll never want to come back to study after a year of relative freedom.

'Is it OK to send e-mails to admissions tutors at universities or will they feel I'm bothering them?'

If a tutor has made their e-mail address available, it's because they want prospective students to contact them. Use this facility wisely, though. Check that your questions are not already answered by their Web site or prospectus.

'How can I find the time to do all this research?'

Start your planning early. If you have just begun an A level, Access or GNVQ course, you need to see how well you cope and how much you enjoy it, but you also need to start your research into the next move. See Checklist 8 in Chapter 7 for a timetable to work to.

An early start means you will be less pressured during the application period, and will have time to make visits and research areas such as sponsorship. The Internet is an excellent tool because, once you know what you are doing, it's quick and efficient and you can build up folders of information tailored to your needs.

You are not on your own!

Your school or college careers coordinators and advisers from the careers centre are there to help. Universities give advice to all students, with particular contacts for school-leavers, mature entrants, those with non-standard qualifications, international students and those with a disability.

If you really feel you don't have time to research your options fully, consider taking a year off. It can be a valuable experience, make you more certain about what you want to do and give you time to find out all the things you need to know.

————————— SITES WORTH SEEING —————————

Note: This section appears at the end of every chapter. For many of the sites referred to in this chapter, see the chapter that deals with that issue in detail. Those listed here are additional sites.

Association of Graduate Recruiters (AGR)

http://agr.csu.man.ac.uk

Press releases have details of surveys into graduate recruitment and salaries.

Internet Detective

http://www.sosig.ac.uk/desire/
internet-detective.html

Web-based tutorial to help you evaluate material from the Internet.

NCH Action For Children: A Parents' Guide to the Internet

http://www.nchafc.org.uk/internet/guide.html

'Children need to learn to be Net-Smart, then they can either avoid potentially risky people or situations, or know what to do if they come across them by accident. To be Net-Smart is an essential skill for the future. The truth is we all need to be Net-Smart, not just our children.' You can download a detailed guide to Internet safety from this site (see Figure 1.11).

Netparents

http://www.netparents.org

American site providing resources for parents concerned about inappropriate material on-line. Lots of useful content and links.

Safe surf

http:www.safesurf.com

An organization working at making the Internet safe for children without censorship. It has developed the Safe Surf Rating System, which you can add to Microsoft's Internet Explorer.

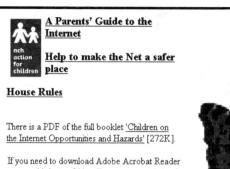

Figure 1.11 It's easy to keep safe if you follow a few basic rules

World Village

http://www.worldvillage.com/wv/school/html/
control.htm

The message here is that empowering and educating parents rather than imposing censorship is the key to protecting children on the Internet. This section of the site gives details of companies involved in finding ways to keep the Internet safe. Much of the software described can be downloaded.

Visa and Mastercard

http://www.visa.com
http://www.mastercard.com

These two major credit card companies have devoted considerable space on their sites to reassuring consumers about the safety of Internet commerce. Both sites have demos and descriptions of how it all works and, not surprisingly, try to persuade you how wonderful Internet shopping is.

Choosing the Right Course

To make an informed choice, you must to have a clear idea of your needs and an overview of the opportunities. This chapter shows how to take a logical approach to assessing yourself and exploring options.

- Self-assessment
- Which subject?
- Which type of course?
- Course searching on the Web
- Special concerns
- Sites worth seeing

SELF-ASSESSMENT

The more alternatives you have, the more organized you need to be in your approach to making a decision. When choosing a higher education course there is a myriad of possibilities. Before you start to explore these you need to look at yourself and answer the following questions.

- What grades am I likely to get in my present subjects?
- Which subjects would I enjoy studying and succeed at?
- Which professions or career areas interest me?

Complete the following checklist and then you'll be ready to move on and look at course options.

CHECKLIST 1: MYSELF
Resources to use
My predicted grades: *Current assessments* *Previous exam grades* *Teachers*
The careers that interest me: *Self-assessment Web sites* *Graduate careers information sites* *Professional bodies' sites*
The subjects I would like/need to study: *Subject gateway Web sites* *Academic discussion groups and mailing lists* *University department Web sites* *Professional bodies' and learned societies' Web sites*

Internet resources

Self-assessment Web sites

To choose a course that will leave the right options open, you need to have thought about what you'd like to do once you've got a degree. It's not essential to know exactly which career you're aiming for at this stage, but you should have an idea of the broad areas that would suit you. There are tools on and off the Web that can help. Some assess your personality, while others match your aptitudes and interests to suitable careers. It's a good idea to use both kinds. Your choice of course and career should be something that suits your personality and uses your abilities and aptitudes.

Going through a process of self-assessment (see Figure 2.1) gives you the information you need to:

- identify careers and courses worth an investment of your time and effort;
- see if your aims are realistic;
- be confident about your suitability for a course or career;
- articulate your strengths, abilities and qualities;
- prepare for applications and interviews.

If you know your good points, it will be easier to convince selectors of your suitability. However, any self-assessment exercise is a snapshot in time, and needs to be repeated as you gain more insight and experience.

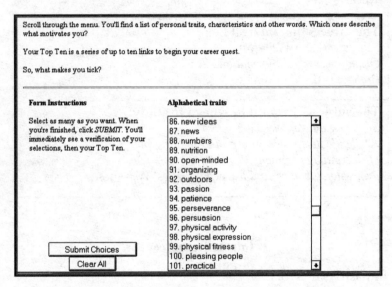

Figure 2.1 If you're not sure which career or study area would suit you take the time to visit Career Quest

Graduate careers information sites

It's never too early to start looking at the career prospects for graduates in your chosen area. Web resources can be used to get an overview of graduate employment and look at current vacancies for graduates from all disciplines (see Figure 2.2).

Your HND in Hospitality Management... What Next?	
Introduction	Going on to Further Study
What Skills have you Gained on your Course	Degree Courses
Jobs Directly Related to Your HND	Vocational Qualifications
Careers Where an HND in Hospitality Management Would Be Useful	Funding
Other Career Areas	Other Options
Who employs Diplomates in Hospitality Management?	Would You Like More Information?

Figure 2.2 Prospects has 'What Next' information for every HND and degree subject

Subject gateway Web sites

Many academic resources on the Web have been grouped by subject in 'gateway' sites. These provide regularly updated links to an enormous number of subject-specific resources. Whatever your interest, you'll find one of these sites is an excellent starting point for an in-depth investigation (see Figure 1.1).

Academic discussion groups and mailing lists

Listen in on academic discussions and take out free 'subscriptions' to mailing lists for subjects that interest you. Mailbase and BUBL – gateways to UK academic mailing lists – are described at the end of this chapter, and general information on newsgroups and mailing lists can be found in the Appendix. Use these resources to see if the prospect of being able to understand the topics and participate in such discussions enthuses you.

University Web sites

These let you take a look inside an institution and its departments. There's detailed information on what to look for in Chapter 3.

Professional bodies' and learned societies' Web sites

See the current concerns for subjects and professions that interest you. Every profession and subject area has one or more Web sites. You'll find careers and vacancy information as well as details of accredited courses. Many educational sites have compiled comprehensive indices of professional bodies and learned societies (see Figure 2.9).

WHICH SUBJECT?

You will have chosen your current A level, GNVQ or other course because you are good at these subjects, enjoy them or need them for the career that attracts you. This process needs to be repeated with your choice of subjects at university. Your options are:

- continuing to study a subject you already know;
- picking up a completely new subject;
- doing a combined or modular degree;
- following a vocational course.

Continuing with a subject you've studied before

Any subject you've already studied can be continued in greater depth at university. Choosing to study a subject for its own sake allows you to keep career options open. If you're not sure whether or not you'd enjoy degree-level study of a familiar subject, use Web-based resources to investigate it in detail.

Choosing a completely new area of study

You can choose to study something completely new, such as philosophy or traditional Chinese medicine. These subjects are taught in a way that assumes no previous knowledge, although they require evidence of interest and aptitude. A virtual look inside a university department can give a feel for a subject and help you decide if its right for you (see Figure 2.3).

Dr Robin Hendry – slides and lecture notes
Overview and glossary of some philosophical terms <u>Notes</u>
Lecture 1 What is Knowledge?: <u>OHP slides, Lecture Notes</u>
Lecture 2 Descartes and Rationalism: <u>OHP slides, Lecture Notes</u>
Lecture 3 Locke and Empiricism: <u>OHP slides, Lecture Notes</u>
Lecture 4 Perceptionand the World I: <u>OHP slides, Lecture Notes</u>
Lecture 5 Perception and the World II: <u>OHP slides, Lecture Notes</u>
Lecture 6 The Problem of Induction I: <u>OHP slides, Lecture Notes</u>
Lecture 7: The Problem of Induction II: <u>OHP slides, Lecture Notes</u>

Figure 2.3   You can investigate all aspects of philosophy at Durham University, including biographical details of staff

Doing a combined or modular degree

See under Which type of course? for details of this type of degree.

Undertaking a vocational qualification

Medicine, dentistry and architecture, for example, are professions that can only be entered with an approved degree in the subject. Use the Web to investigate entry requirements for all professions. Some vocational degree courses, such as accountancy and law, are not essential prerequisites for entry to those professions, but give exemptions from future study and exams.

WHICH TYPE OF COURSE?

Higher education courses are of the following types:

- single-subject degree;
- combined studies/modular degree;
- degree that confers qualified teacher status (QTS);
- Higher National Diploma (HND);
- Diploma of Higher Education (Dip HE);
- sandwich;
- Foundation or Year Zero;
- franchised.

Many courses have part-time or distance learning options. If these are important factors for you, check the availability of flexible study at an early stage. Look at the Credit Accumulation and Transfer (CAT) section of the university's Web site.

Single-subject degrees

These allow you to study a subject in depth. Many single-subject courses offer the possibility of taking subsidiary courses, such as a language, IT or management. Subsidiary subjects are studied in less detail and not included in the title of the degree awarded. Most degree courses in England and Wales are honours degrees, leading to a Bachelor of Arts (BA) or Bachelor of Science (BSc). Some vocational degrees take their title from their vocational area – engineering is BEng, medicine is BMed and education is BEd, for example.

Combined studies/modular degree

This kind of degree gives you the opportunity to study more than one subject, such as maths and computing, journalism and French. Subjects can be given equal weighting or done as a major/minor combination. Some modular courses allow you to combine more than two subjects. It often looks as if you can combine almost any subjects, but timetabling and other constraints mean there are limitations. Every university organizes its combined studies programme in a different way, so course details need to be checked carefully.

The advantages of doing a combined degree course are that:

- there is the chance to gain expertise and knowledge in more than one area;
- some combinations go well together, such as business studies and a foreign language;
- it allows you to keep your options open;
- it's a way of exploring a new subject area while retaining links with a known one;
- you can construct a course tailored to your needs and interests;
- it can help you demonstrate a range of skills when applying for employment.

There are possible disadvantages too:

- employers may feel it does not give you enough specialist knowledge;
- the level of study in a subject may not be sufficient for entry to certain professions, such as psychology.

Higher National Diploma (HND)

HND courses have a strong vocational bias. They have lower entry requirements than degree courses and are usually a year shorter. Many students use them as a stepping stone to a degree course. One-year 'top up' courses convert HNDs to degrees in subject areas such as business studies and computing. Many degree courses accept HND students on the second year of a degree and some institutions market their HNDs as 2+2 courses, with easy progression to the last two years of a related degree after two years' HND study.

Students completing HND courses can find themselves at a disadvantage when competing with graduates for jobs. Some, however, find that employers are positive about the very practical nature of their study. A recent AGCAS survey found that nearly 90 per cent of HND diplomates had gone on to study for a degree or found work six months after completing their course (reported in *What do Graduates Do?*, AGCAS, 1999).

Diploma of Higher Education (Dip HE)

These are similar to HNDs and are available in a range of subjects, including nursing, housing studies, social work, youth and community work.

Sandwich course

Degrees and HNDs done as sandwich courses have part of the course – usually a year – as a work placement. It is normal for sandwich students to be paid around 75 per cent of the graduate starting salary during that year and to undertake work related to their study. The experience period is assessed and counts towards the qualification.

Many students mistakenly believe that sandwich courses are only available for science and engineering disciplines. The opportunity to have an industrial placement as part of your degree is now open to students from most disciplines. (See Figure 2.4) Examples include:

- sociology or psychology at Brunel;
- wildlife conservation at the University of East London;
- fashion at Central St Martin's.

As well as improving your future employment prospects, these courses can ease some of your financial problems!

Foundation or Year Zero courses

Such courses offer an introduction to degree-level study for students who:

- made the wrong choice of A levels or equivalent;
- got poor results;
- are returning to study after a long break.

The ASET directory contains information about sandwich courses at universities and colleges in the UK and is published once a year. We are also making some of the information available on these pages.

Each course is listed in one, and only one, section even though some courses could, with some justification, be put in more than one section.

The sections in the directory are:

Art, Design and Peforming Arts	Humanities
Built Environment	Maths, IT and Computing
Business and Management	Science
Engineering and Technology	Social Sciences

Within each section universities and colleges are listed in alphabetical order, followed by all of their courses in that section.

Figure 2.4   The ASET database gives an overview of sandwich courses

They are mainly for those wanting to study science and engineering. Successful completion allows progression to a related degree.

Franchised courses

Many colleges of further education offer degree courses on a franchise basis from a 'parent' university. These give students a wider range of opportunities locally than would otherwise be the case. Franchised courses have the same syllabus and assessment methods as the parent course, and the end qualification is awarded by the university. However, students on franchised courses may not have access to the same range of learning resources (library, computers, specialized laboratories) and in some cases may need to go to the university to complete the course. Use the Web sites of the local college and linked university to check details and compare facilities and resources.

COURSE SEARCHING ON THE WEB
UCAS course search

Once you know the subject(s) and type of course you want to do, Web-based course search sites will help you produce lists that match your criteria. The best starting point for this is the UCAS site (see Figure 2.5), which is regularly updated and offers free access to all users. It enables you to search for courses by entering:

- subject titles or choosing from a list of 600 broad areas;
- course level – this includes degrees, diplomas, HNDs or all levels;
- where you want to study;
- entry requirements that reflect your qualifications.

Search For: The search is based on the title words of courses offered by Higher Education institutions in the UK. You can type up to 3 words into the box (eg applied chemistry law) or you can pick them from this list.	Sport
Choose A Course Level	Degree
Choose A Region If you want to limit your search to institutions in a particular region you may do so here. If not leave the option open at all regions.	North West
Choose Entry Requirements Select the entry requirements you would like to see with the results of your search.	☐ A-level ☒ BTEC ☐ GNVQ ☐ International Baccalaureate ☐ Scottish Higher ☐ Scottish National
	Search Clear

Figure 2.5 The UCAS web site has a simple, effective search facility

Entry requirements

Unless you have chosen a specialized subject, such as prosthetics, it's likely that you will now have a long list from which you need to eliminate unsuitable courses. The first thing to check is entry requirements. The list produced using the UCAS course search facility (see Figure 2.5) enables you to do this quickly. Clicking on a course title will give you its entry requirements (see Figure 2.6). Clicking on the name of the university will take you to e-mail and Web links that enable you to do more in-depth research (see Figure 2.7).

Check that:

- subjects you have studied are acceptable in terms of entry requirements;
- grades asked for are not well above or below those predicted for you.

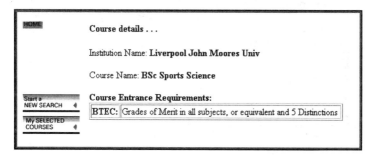

Figure 2.6 You can see entry requirements by clicking on the course title

It is relatively simple to see if you match the requirements in terms of A levels, BTEC, International Baccalaureate or GNVQs, but more difficult for a non-standard entrant. Many courses will include an encouraging statement along the lines of 'we welcome applications from students without standard entry requirements who can demonstrate that they will benefit from this course'. In these circumstances, e-mail the admissions tutor with details of your qualifications and experience to check how acceptable these would be. See Chapter 3 for details of how to find addresses of specific members of staff at a university.

Investigating course titles

Some courses have imaginative or obscure titles that do not make their content clear. The results from a UCAS course search may contain courses that would not have attracted your attention. A Joint Honours BSc can prove to have surprising possibilities!

Courses with the same title can have very different content. A degree in English, sports studies, business or computer science at one university can have little in common with a similarly titled course at another. You need to compare detailed descriptions of modules, options and specialisms. University departmental Web pages are excellent sources of information for this (see Chapter 3).

Liverpool John Moores University
Recruitment Team, Roscoe Court, 4 Rodney Street,
Liverpool, L1 2TZ
Tel: 0151 231 5090/5091
Fax: 0151 231 3194
Email: recruitment@livjm.ac.uk
Website: http://www.livjm.ac.uk/

Campus Locations
Over twenty teaching/learning buildings throughout the city. IM Marsh campus is four miles from city centre.
Accommodation
Percentage of first years requiring accommodation who can be accommodated in institution managed accommodation: 70
Estimated weekly cost of institution-managed accommodation for 39 weeks: (no food) £39.50–£48.00
Overseas opportunities
Number of students on a placement or study period abroad: 80
Interviewing
No policy of interviewing except for Teaching, Pharmacy, courses requiring auditions and mature applicants.
Open Days
Individual departments have Open Days. The 'JMU Experience' takes place on 8 July and 23 September. Further details from the Enquiry Helpline.

Figure 2.7 The university link from the UCAS course list

Choosing the Right Course

The UCAS lists give links to:

- outline course information;
- basic institutional details, including accommodation costs and open day details;
- university Web sites for courses listed;
- an e-mail address for prospectus requests.

Nursing courses

Entry to nursing can be via a degree or diploma. Degrees in nursing can be found using the UCAS course search. Applications for diploma courses in England and Scotland are made using other application systems – NMAS and CATCH respectively. In Wales, applications for nursing diplomas are made to individual institutions. Full details are given in Chapter 7. Information on all nursing courses at diploma level can be found on the NMAS, CATCH and Welsh Nursing Board Web sites, which are listed at the end of this chapter.

Books and CDs

You should find a good selection of publications that compare and evaluate courses in your school, college or careers centre library. When using books, check the date of publication to see how current the information is. Courses, their content and entry requirements change from year to year. It's a good idea to use Web-based information alongside books to be sure you have the most up-to-date information.

CD-based course search programs that are subscription services face a challenge from the free Web-based information. One advantage they have over the Web is their consistency. The material is presented in a standard format and they're not prone to the delays that you can encounter with the Web. However, these programs do not have the same detail and depth of information, nor are they always as up to date as the best Web sites. In some cases, CD programs supplement the information on disk with Web links to university and professional bodies' sites. You will find programs such as ECCTIS

Course Discover, Higher Ideas and Headlight in your local careers library.

SPECIAL CONCERNS

Most universities actively encourage students with special educational needs arising from physical, sensory or learning disabilities. If you have the potential to cope with academic work, your disability should not be a barrier. There is a range of well-established support mechanisms for students with disabilities and the scope of these can be investigated using the Internet. Each chapter in this book has a section highlighting concerns of students with special needs and providing details of Internet-based resources that can help.

For people with disabilities, the Internet has the potential to remove barriers to education and to researching and arranging suitable provision. It enables you to communicate with others who have faced and resolved your problem, and benefit from their experience. Many organizations use the new communication technologies to promote, publicize and develop strategies for making higher education a place of truly equal opportunities. Details of software that enhances computer accessibility can be found in the Appendix.

When you have completed the checklist below, you're ready to move on to looking at the finer points of choosing the right course.

CHECKLIST 2: INITIAL COURSE EVALUATION

Web resources to use

Subject:

Typical entry requirements:
UCAS course search

Areas of study/specialisms include:
Universities' departmental pages

Why I'm keen to do it:
Mailbase

Career opportunities:
Graduate careers guidance sites
Professional bodies' Web sites
Subject gateway

Can be combined with:
UCAS course search

Sandwich courses available?
ASET courses database

Need for accreditation/recognition?
Professional bodies' Web sites

SITES WORTH SEEING

Self-assessment

As there is little freely accessible material available on the Web that relates to self-assessment for higher education in the UK, the resources listed below are from other countries. They are a good starting point for self-assessment, regardless of where you live. Subscription services designed for UK students may be available through your school, college or local careers centre and include programs such as Discourse, Centigrade and Course Finder.

INTEC

http://www.intec.edu.za/career/career.htm
South African college offering free on-line access and scoring of an interest inventory/personality test called CareerMatch. Six of your most significant personality attributes are matched against similar profiles for 100 different careers.

Schoolfinder

http://www.schoolfinder.com/career/carquiz/htm/
Canadian site that provides an interest quiz that can be completed and scored online.

Youth Works Career Quest Pride

http://www.youthworks.ca/yw-pride.htm
The 'Top 10 Checklist' section of this Canadian site has a list of personal traits and characteristics (see Figure 2.1). Choose those that describe what motivates you and, in return, get a list of job areas that suit your personality. The detailed training information relates to Canada, but the job areas covered are common to most countries.

Subject gateway sites

BUBL

http://www.bubl.ac.uk

This site acts as an information service for the UK academic community. There are links from here to sites dealing with all subjects, journals, mailing lists and much more.

Pinakes

http://www.hw.ac.uk/libWWW/irn/pinakes/
pinakes.html

The Pinakes was a catalogue for the Library of Alexandria, once regarded as a universal store of knowledge. This site (see Figure 2.8), a gateway to the gateways, aims to do the same for the academic Internet – today's universal store of knowledge.

PINAKES: Subject List

Aerospace ~ Agriculture ~ Architecture Art ~ Biomedicine ~ Botany ~ Business/Economics ~ Chemistry ~ Computer Science ~ Conflict ~ Design ~ Development ~ Economics/Business Education ~ Engineering ~ Environment ~ Food Science ~ Forestry ~ General ~ History ~ Humanities ~ Information/Libraries ~ Interdisciplinary ~ Languages/Linguistics ~ Law ~ Libraries/Information ~ Mathematics ~ Medicine ~ Multi-Subject ~ Philosophy ~ Physics ~ Psychology ~ Science ~ Social Science ~ Urban Design ~ Veterinary Science

---

Figure 2.8   All human knowledge is here!

Academic discussion groups and mailing lists

Mailbase

http://www.mailbase.ac.uk

This site provides over 2000 electronic discussion lists for the UK higher education community (see Figure A.10). You can use the lists to look at what is being discussed in your subject area. Mailing lists are not just subject-specific, they also deal with wider issues, such as disability. The Directory of Scholarly and Professional e-conferences – which evaluates and organizes the world's academically oriented discussion lists, newsgroups, mailing lists and chat groups — can be linked to from Mailbase (http://www.mailbase.ac.uk/kovacs).

Course databases

Association for Sandwich Education (ASET)

http://www.edu.coventry.ac.uk/aset

Here you can find a database of sandwich courses with links to detailed information (see Figure 2.4).

Central Council for Education and Training in Social Work (CCETSW)

http://www.ccetsw.org.uk

Careers information and details of social work training courses are to be found here. Application for social work degrees is through UCAS, for diplomas through the Social Work Application System (SWAS). SWAS packs can be ordered from the UCAS Web site. The CCETSW is to be replaced by a new National Training Organization (NTO). Details of all NTOs can be found at http://www.nto-nc.org

Nursing Board for Scotland (NBS)

http://www.nbs.org.uk

Nurses and Midwives Admissions Service (NMAS)

http://www.nmas.ac.uk

Choosing the Right Course

Nursing Board for Wales (NBW)
http://www.wnb.org.uk

University Central Admissions Service (UCAS)
http://www.ucas.ac.uk
For details of all the above, see Chapter 7.

Prospectus information

NISS – UK Campus Information Services
http://www.niss.ac.uk/education/hesites/cwis.html
An alphabetical list of links to all UK Higher Education Institutions is available at this site. During the clearing period (see Chapter 7), you can use these links for direct access to universities' clearing pages.

UK Universities Sensitive Map
http://scitsc.wlv.ac.uk/ukinfo/uk.map.html
For map and text links to all universities and colleges in the UK, look no further. The latest version incorporates the ability to choose a topic and go directly to that section of the chosen university Web site. Topics include undergraduate prospectus, academic departments, students' union, international students, British council profile, teaching assessment and contact information.

Graduate careers information

Each university has its own careers service. You can compare them using their Web sites. In addition, a growing number of sites offer general guidance to graduates. One of the most established and respected is Prospects.

Prospects
http://www.prospects.csu.ac.uk
The Careers Services Unit (CSU) collects and disseminates information on graduate recruitment in the UK. It provides a link between employers, university careers services and

graduate job seekers. The whole site is worth looking at, but, at this stage, the section entitled 'What can I do with my degree/HND in ...' is of particular value (see Figure 2.2).

Others to look at
http://www.eurograduate.com
http://www.gradunet.co.uk
http://www.gti.co.uk
http://www.topgrads.co.uk

Professional bodies and societies

The Scholarly Societies Project
http://www.lib.uwaterloo.ca/society/
overview.html
Lists and provides links to scholarly societies around the world (see Figure 2.9).

Subject Area	Number of Societies
Agricultural and Food Sciences	45
Anthropology	42
Archaeology	23
Architecture	49
Area Studies & Time-Period Studies NEW	39
Astronomy	30
Bibliography & History of the Book	4
Biology	180
Business	22
Chemistry & Chemical Engineering	208
Civil Engineering	134
Classical Studies	16
Communication & Media Studies	19
Computer Science	151
Dance	7

Figure 2.9 The Scholarly Societies Project provides links to over 1200 organizations, covering most areas of academic study in all countries

Choosing the Right Course

National Information Services and Systems (NISS), Professional page

http://www.niss.ac.uk/education/prof_bodies.html

Links to the Web sites of professional bodies, learned societies, staff associations and similar organizations are available at this site. Use these to explore career or subject areas, check entry requirements and degree accreditation.

Note: The sites listed below are examples of what is available. To find a similar resource for your subject area, use the related gateway from NISS, Pinakes or The Scholarly Societies Project.

Association for Medical Education (ASME)

http://www.asme.org.uk

The Association maintains a compendium of UK undergraduate medical courses, updated annually, that gives basic course details.

British Psychological Society

http://www.bps.org.uk

Comprehensive information is available here for those considering a career in psychology, including a database of undergraduate psychology courses in the UK and the Republic of Ireland, which confer eligibility for Graduate Membership and/or the Graduate Basis for Registration on completion. This is essential for entry to further professional training leading to chartered psychologist training.

Council for British Archaeology

http://www.britarch.ac.uk/index.html

Everything you would ever wish to know about archaeology, including information on courses, breaking news, events and exhibitions, grants and awards.

Environment Council

http://www.greenchannel.com/tec/doec/search.htm

This is a searchable database of academic, professional and vocational courses related to the environment. It includes subjects such as civil engineering and archaeology as well as environmental science.

Institute of Electrical Engineers

http://www.iee.org.uk

Careers information and an annually updated list of accredited degree courses in electrical, electronic, computer and manufacturing engineering can be found here. This list can be downloaded as a Word document from the site.

National Council for the Training of Journalists (NCTJ)

http://www.itecharlow.co.uk/nctj

Comprehensive information is provided on careers in journalism, together with a list of courses at all levels approved by the NCTJ.

Particle Physics and Astronomy Research Council (PPARC)

http://www.pparc.ac.uk/role/astrouni.html

List of, and links to, UK universities with courses in astronomy, astrophysics and planetary science.

Royal Institute of British Architects (RIBA)

http://www.riba.org

The 'Practice and education' section has a list of, and links to, schools of architecture in the UK, with courses recognized for exemption from the RIBA Examination in Architecture.

sites worth seeing

Choosing the Right Place

This chapter is a guide to use of the Web for detailed course and place research. Take a virtual look at general university facilities, specific departmental information and investigate the surrounding area.

- General university information
- Scottish higher education
- Student support services
- Departmental information
- Special concerns
- Partnerships
- Student life
- Open days
- Sites worth seeing

Once you have a preliminary short list of courses, you can start to investigate each in depth. University Web sites enable you to compare courses and institutions and reassure yourself that what they offer is right for you, and that you are right for them.

About the University
The University
Publications

Study Opportunities
Prospectuses
Admissions and Open Days
How to Apply

Campus Information
News
Diary
Administration

Schools and Departments
Departmental Homepages

How to find us
Visiting the University
Maps

Services we offer
Campus Services
Conferences
Alumni Information
Media Information

Contacting the University

Who to Contact
Email Addresses
Telephone Numbers

The City and Region
Birmingham

Index

Search

Figure 3.1 University home pages act as signposts to the information on the site

GENERAL UNIVERSITY INFORMATION

Every university Web site has a mix of marketing and academic material. To fully research your choices, you need to look at both. In a few cases, access to departmental and other academic content is restricted to internal users only. However, many universities recognize the value of letting the wider public see more than overtly promotional details and make a range of material available to all users.

Facts and figures

Introductory pages – such as that shown in Figure 3.2 – summarize key points about the university. They will often include historical information and details of the type of university. Universities can be old or new, large or small, on a compact campus or spread across a city. You have to decide which kind will suit you best.

Teaching Assessment
The University's achievement in teaching is subject to external assessment by panels of assessors appointed by the Higher Education Funding Council for England. Under the former teaching assessment system, by which teaching in University departments was rated as excellent, satisfactory or unsatisfactory, the following 6 Departments were rated 'Excellent': English Law, Mechanical Engineering, Chemistry, Geography and Social Work. Under the present system, teaching and learning is rated out of a total possible score of 24. Any score above 18 is rated excellent. No Bristol department has scored less than 20. The following scores have been achieved: Sociology 21, Russian, 20, Hispanic, Portuguese and Latin American Studies 22, French 20, German 21, Italian 21 and Civil Engineering, Electrical and Electronic Engineering 24, History of Art 20, Aerospace Engineering 22, Drama Theatre, Film Television 23.
Student Admissions
The University is committed to the promotion of equal opportunities and welcomes applications from candidates of all social and ethnic backgrounds, including overseas students. Contact Admissions Office, tel: (0117) 928 7678, email: admissions@bristol.ac.uk
http/www.bris.ac.uk/Depts/Registrar/Admissions/
Entrance Standards
Entrance standards for Bristol are high, but all students are admitted on the basis of an assessment of their academic promise. Students from educationally deprived backgrounds are admitted on lower absolute A-level scores. On a basis of 3 A-levels (A=10, B=8, C=6 etc), the average entrance scores for 1997 were:

Arts 26.2	Engineering 26.3
Science 26.0	Law 26.7
Medicine 28.7	Social Sciences 26.1

Staff statistics
The University is the ninth largest employer in the West of England
Academic 1,326
Research 699
Support 1,260
Total (full-time) 3,285
Total (including part-time) 4,688
Students
Undergraduates 9,494
Postgraduates 2,117
Men 6,012
Women 5,599
Destinations of last year's graduates
Permanent appointments 49%
Research, further academic study and training 25%
Travel/year off/deferred offer/overseas returners/others 7%
Temporary appointments 6%
Seeking work 3%
Unknown 10%

Figure 3.2 Bristol University's facts and figures page gives an overview of the university's characteristics and strengths

Prospectuses

All universities have their prospectuses online. Some are just a copy of the paper version, but more often they contain, or link to, detailed information. You can normally browse through a prospectus or conduct a specific search, saving the information found to disk. The prospectus will give you course outlines, details of entry requirements and open days. Course and admissions tutors may make their e-mail addresses available and encourage contact from students who have questions not answered elsewhere. There may be an alternative prospectus produced by the students' union.

Quality assessments

All university departments and courses have been, or will be, assessed by one of the Higher Education Funding Councils. Assessment reports show how each subject provider meets the aims and objectives it has set itself. These reports are published on the Internet as well as on paper and are used as an evaluation tool by prospective students and employers. Many universities include details on their Web site (see Figure 3.2), particularly where the findings were complimentary!

You need to be cautious when making judgements about a university based on its assessment report. It should form part, but not all, of your evaluation of a course and institution. More information on how to find and use such reports is given in Chapter 4.

Financial considerations

Universities are very conscious of students' financial worries and use their sites to give information on money matters. This can include advice on likely costs, help with budgeting, suggestions for ways of saving and earning money, as well as details of financial and practical help, such as the following:

● **Access funds** Available for some students whose studies are affected by financial hardship. As this applies to more students than the funds can help, there are generally criteria for eligibility.

- **Scholarships and bursaries** Some universities offer their own scholarships. Others will help you research sources of additional funding.
- **Job shops** These act as employment agencies for students, helping them find term-time and vacation work in the university or surrounding community.

For other ways to improve your financial situation while at university, see Chapter 5.

Learning resources

Facilities to support learning vary from institution to institution. Financial constraints have placed pressure on resources and in some cases led to charges for using them. When universities are assessed, their learning resources are reported on (see Chapter 4).

Use the university's Web site to check details of library, computing, laboratory and workshop facilities and what costs are associated with them. Points to check include:

- ratio of students to equipment;
- costs for computer use/printing;
- opening times of libraries and computer facilities;
- availability in holiday periods;
- availability of material via the university intranet;
- age of computing, laboratory and workshop equipment;
- arrangements for Internet and e-mail use.

SCOTTISH HIGHER EDUCATION

If you intend to study in Scotland, there are significant differences you need to be aware of. The Scottish Office site is a good starting point for finding out what these are (see Figure 3.3). It has links to every university and college Web site.

First Degree Courses

In Scotland, degrees are awarded for the successful completion of a 3 year full-time course at an appropriate level (an Ordinary degree) or a 4 year course at a more specialised and demanding level (an Honours degree). Degrees in Medicine, Dentistry, Architecture, Veterinary Science and in a few other areas can take up to six years in length.

In the four oldest universities, the first degree in the Arts, Humanities and Languages is called Master of Arts (MA). Other higher education institutions in Scotland offer degrees with the title Bachelor. The universities and two of the other institutions (Queen Margaret College and the Royal Scottish Academy of Music and Drama) have powers to award their own degrees; the remainder have valida-tion arrangements with another educational institution.

Higher National Certificates and Diplomas, usually taken in further educational colleges, may lead to degrees, in technical or scientific subjects. HNC courses normally last one year and most HND courses 2 years, if taken full-time. HNC and HND awards are made by the Scottish Vocational Education Council.

Many courses, especially in science and engineering, are of the 'sandwich' variety, with students spending periods of professional training or work experience in a professional or industrial environment. Such courses normally take a year longer to complete than full-time courses.

Courses for intending teachers are offered at undergraduate level leading to the BEd degree, and at post-graduate level leading to the Post-graduate Certificate in Education (PGCE).

Figure 3.3   The Scottish Office site gives an overview of the system

Financial implications of taking a longer course

Scottish degree courses are, on average, a year longer than those in other parts of the UK. The new financial arrange-ments for students have led to some interesting anomalies with regard to this. Currently, students who live in Scotland or any member state of the EU, excluding England, Wales and Northern Ireland, do not pay fees for the extra year. However, if students from England, Wales or Northern Ireland choose to study in Scotland, they have to pay fees for each year of their studies. All students have to cover living expenses for a longer period than elsewhere.

The fees situation may change. The best sources of information are the sites dealing with fees and loans listed at the end of Chapter 5.

Entry requirements

There is a great deal of flexibility in Scottish higher education (see Figure 3.4). Second-year entry to some degree courses is possible – particularly for those with good A levels – and this can be an attractive option for those worried about financial pressures. However, this takes away the opportunity to do a broad first year and try out different subjects before deciding on a final choice of degree. Coming in to an established group where friendships have been made is also a worry for some students.

UK and international entry requirements are fully discussed in 'Entry from School' and 'normally expected' entry grades are given in relation to all courses. It is important to bear in mind:

- Scottish Higher grade qualifications are the basis for the four-year Honours degree course. Entry may be from 5th or 6th year. Very good Highers and SYS passes may enable entry direct to Second Year.
- GCE A-levels provide two entry routes: High grades may enable entry to the Second Year of most courses, making the Honours course of three years' duration and there is the added flexibility, with less high grades, of entry to First Year.
- Other qualifications, notably those gained in Further Education, provide well-recognised 'mainstream' entry routes. Overall 15% of our entrants (25% in Engineering) gained admission last year on the basis of qualifications including SCOTVEC and BTEC vocational and modular elements, recognised 'Access' courses, HNC and HND. Again, entry is flexible to the appropriate point of degree courses. Often FE qualifications enable entry to Second Year and sometimes to Third Year.
- The University is keeping abreast of current developments under the Higher Still Programme and will review its Admissions requirements as further information on these new qualifications is made available. Students who require further information to inform their future course of study should direct their enquiries to the Admissions Office in the first instance.

Figure 3.4 Heriot Watt in common with other Scottish Universities has detailed advice on flexible entry

Ordinary or Honours degree?

After their second year, students in Scotland can choose to do an Ordinary or Honours degree. That choice is usually dictated by academic performance. Ordinary degrees, which offer a broad-based qualification, are chosen by around 25 per cent of students.

Professional recognition of qualifications

All UK professional bodies recognize Scottish degrees, but there are two subject areas that have additional requirements for wider recognition:

- **Law** The Scottish legal system differs from the rest of the UK and degrees in Scottish law qualify graduates for work within it. To be recognized in the rest of the UK, it is necessary to do a conversion course, which has a cost attached to it. Some universities offer courses in English and Scottish law.
- **Teaching** The Scottish teaching qualification is recognized throughout the UK – there is no need for additional study. Teachers trained outside Scotland need to satisfy the requirements of, and register with, the Scottish General Teaching Council. It is unlawful for a Scottish education authority to employ a teacher in a public-sector nursery, primary, special or secondary school who is not registered with the Council (see Figure 3.5). If your long-term aim is to teach in Scotland, it can be simpler to train there.

Other considerations

The locations of Scottish universities give students the opportunity to live in a city but have spectacular countryside on their doorstep. If you're a keen skier, there are several universities within easy reach of ski slopes!

Registering to teach in Scotland

If you wish to teach in an education authority school in Scotland, you are required to register with the General Teaching Council for Scotland.

Requests for information about the availability of teaching posts in Scotland should be addressed to the relevant local authority education office.

- What about Registration? (General information)
- Applications for Registration from Teachers Qualified in England, Wales and Northern Ireland
- Applications for Registration from Teachers Qualified in European Union Countries and Overseas
- Further Education Lecturers: Registration and Probation Arrangements
- Information about probation
- Record of service forms
- Scottish local authority addresses
- Useful addresses

Figure 3.5 The GTC Web site allows you to check registration details

STUDENT SUPPORT SERVICES

There is a range of services to help make your life at university run smoothly.

Accommodation services

You will normally have the option of living in university-owned properties or be given help with finding other rented accommodation (see Figure 3.6). University accommodation offices may inspect and approve private-sector properties to ensure safe and reasonable housing for students. Many universities offer all first-year students guaranteed accommodation. Costs and facilities can vary enormously. Computer links that connect you to the university network are a feature of newer properties, but the more facilities you have, the more you pay.

Every year Housing Service publishes a booklet called Home from Home which details student accommodation at the University of Sheffield. This booklet can be obtained from the above address or its content browsed via the Internet by selecting the button or text below:

- Introduction
- University self-catering properties
- □ flats
- □ houses
- Halls of Residence
- Housing for graduate students
- Private housing
- Other Information
- □ married students and families
- □ students with a disability
- □ mature students
- □ nursing students
- □ parking
- □ telephones
- How to apply for accommodation
- Location Maps

Figure 3.6 Accommodation details are a feature of most university Web sites

The careers service

It may seem strange to look at the help you'll be offered when leaving university before you've even started, but it's never too early to compare the careers services of your preferred universities. After all you'll be using them to help you get the job that will repay the investment you made in yourself.

University careers services do more than just help you find jobs in your final year. It's worth investigating the services they offer, both to current and former students. These can include:

- career-specific courses, such as an introduction to management;

- application workshops, such as assessment centre skills, psychometric testing;
- job shops that help you find temporary work while studying;
- recruitment events – see which employers regularly recruit through them;
- access to interest inventories;
- personal careers interviews;
- comprehensive careers libraries with occupational and employer information;
- vacancy listings;
- mentor schemes (see Figure 3.7);
- destination details for previous students.

Some careers services password protect access to sections of their site, such as current vacancies, to restrict this to their own students. It's worth checking that, as a former student, you will be able to access current information after you've graduated.

Destination statistics

You need to know what has happened to other people who did the course you're looking at. A university's destination statistics are normally collated by its careers service and available on its site or departmental pages (see Figure 3.8).

DEPARTMENTAL INFORMATION

Most university Web sites allow some access to their departmental pages. These are a resource for existing students and used to disseminate information and communicate within the department. They also act as a showcase for the work of a department. They are an excellent way of seeing what it's like to study a subject in a particular place (see Figure 3.9). It's not fair to judge a department by its Web pages alone, but they are an excellent starting point for further investigation.

<u>Careerlink</u>
One of the most helpful sources of information and advice is to talk to a graduate who is doing the type of work which interests you. We have developed a contacts scheme whereby we can put you in touch with UEA graduates and other professionals who are willing to help in some way. If you give details of the kind of work which interests you, we will send you information about the scheme if an appropriate contact is available.

JE
is an independent business consultant and has a wide experience of hotel and catering and the tourism industry and of vocational education throughout western and parts of eastern Europe. He can also offer advice on funding for European mobility schemes. Teacher training placements may be available. John runs a business importing yachts, teaches for the OBS, is a part-time adviser for BTEC and a RYA racing coach. Please write, phone or e-mail.

JD
currently works as an in-house marketing officer for the National Trust. She started her career in a PR consultancy and has also worked as a press and public relations officer for a sollege of further and higher education. Please write or phone.

MV
has nearly 20 years' experience working in several European countries with the World Health Organisation and the United Nations, including international conference work. Her current job is in Geneva as technical officer for WHO's new annual publication, The World Health Report. Please write or fax to home address in France for advice on working conditions in international organisations of the UN system, and in France, Switzerland, Denmark.

PC
is a principal factory inspector. A graduate in microbiology, he joined the Health and Safety Executive in 1979. During his probationary training he obtained a postgraduate disploma in occupational health and safety. He has worked with docks, chemicals, food, entertainment and general manufacturing, obtaining a wide experience in many health and safety issues. Currently he manages a team of six inspectors covering the engineering andutilities sectors.

Figure 3.7 The University of East Anglia's Careerlink scheme is open to current and former students

Some of the best departmental Web sites give detailed timetable information, lecture notes, reading lists, copies of previous exam papers, details of current student projects and links to related resources (see Figure 2.3). The more you can see into a department the more you are able to judge whether it will be right for you.

Each year, we collect information about our our students' "First Destinations". We ask them to tell us what they are doing six months after their graduation.

You can see the information about those who graduated in several ways:

🔍 **Search for a course by name**

🏛 **The University of Manchester - Overall Statistics**

- **First Degree Students**
  - ○ Total
  - ○ Male Students
  - ○ Female Students
- **Postgraduate Students**
  - ○ Total
- **First Degree Students by Faculty**
  - ○ Arts
  - ○ Economics
  - ○ Education
  - ○ Law
  - ○ Medicine
  - ○ Dental School
  - ○ Science
  - ○ Biological Science
- **Type of Employment**

Figure 3.8 Destination figures for Manchester students are easy to find and use

Harwinder Padda

First year Physics with Studies in North America

"I was originally on the Physics with Computing course but I have just changed to Physics with North American Studies. I am still continuing with my computational options, though. I chose Salford because of the course and when I came to the Open Day the laser applications demonstration was quite amazing and that clinched it. I also liked the way the place [Salford University] is set out. As a city, Manchester is very good socially and caters for many different tastes. The year in America gives you another angle and experiencing another country and culture helps you with job prospects. The course is very intense but enjoyable"

Email: h.padda@physics.salford.ac.uk

Figure 3.9 If you're considering physics at Salford, you're encouraged to e-mail present students to find out what it's really like

---

Educational Sites

- **Prosthetics and Orthotics at Salford University**

- **National Centre for Training & Education in Prosthetics & Orthotics**

- **UK Prosthetics Forum Links Page**

- **Biomech-L**

- **Biomechanics World Wide Class Homepages**

- **Orthotics and Prosthetics Online**

- **Biomechanics World Wide**

- **Northwest Orthotics and Prosthetics**

- **Advanced Bio-mechanics and Prosthetics Information**

- **Web Quiz**

- **CAD/CAM Orthotics**

- **CAD/CAM-Systems in Pedorthics, Prosthetics & Orthotics**

- **The Association for Children with Hand or Arm Deficiency**

Figure 3.10   Use a department's Web site to help you research an area new to you

Most departments act as mini-gateways to subject or vocational information (see Figure 3.10). Use these to help you construct a strong application and prepare for interview.

Staff information

The most important resource for learners is the staff who teach them. As well as giving current information on staff–student ratios, departmental Web sites allow you to find out about the individuals who could be teaching you. How a course is taught is affected by the interests, expertise and enthusiasms of the person delivering it. Many lecturers have Web pages that describe their interests and link to their publications (see Figure 3.11). It's useful to know what those are. In addition to giving you something to talk about at an interview, it's a good idea to go on a course where the research interests of the staff match your own.

Staff and Research Areas

Professors of Social Policy

Tim Booth BA PhD, Chair of Department
Three key themes run through his research work: an interest in the relation between research and policy; a concern with the links between policy and outcomes; and a focus on the impact of social change on individual welfare. A recurring topic of investigation has been the interplay of environment and behaviour as revealed in studies of the relationship between institutional environments and the outcomes of care, the policy environment and the utilisation of research by policy makers, and the social environment and the experience of disability. His current research is in the field of parenting by people with learning difficulties. He teaches on both the undergraduate and postgraduate programmes.

For further information visit my Homepage

Figure 3.11   University staff often have personal Web pages with biographical details. This is from the Sociology Department at Sheffield University

SPECIAL CONCERNS

Well thought out and accessibly designed pages are a good indication that the university has experience of students with disabilities and has considered their needs (see Figure 1.10). A university that does not provide all this information on its Web site may still provide the services and support you require, so don't exclude those with poor information from your initial research. Instead, e-mail them and ask for details and contact information, including e-mail addresses for students who share your needs and would be willing to communicate with you. Find out how they coped with the challenges, and how they rate the support they've had.

There are resources on the Web that can help you find the right questions to ask and the right people to contact. The checklist for disabled students produced by the European Commission (Figure 3.12) is intended for use by students investigating study in other member states, but the down-loadable text file is useful whether or not you want to go overseas as part of your course.

STUDYING ABROAD

Volume 1: Checklist of needs for students with disabilities

Preface
Students with disabilities, contemplating studying overseas, might want to obtain some idea of the sort of facilities available at the host university. It is best to get into contact beforehand with the people responsible for these matters. The aim of this checklist is to make the task that much easier.

Instructions for use
1. It is important to take great care in listing needs so that the information received is as accurate as possible. For this purpose, you should first read the checklist (in your own language) and tick the item that mentions the information you seek or the requirements you need.
2. After questions and requirements have been listed in your own language, using the checklist as the basis, you will find it easy to find the same items in the questionnaire in the language of the host university, and tick these. There is therefore no need for you to translate any of the questions yourself. The completed list may be sent to the host university.
3. Checklists can be downloaded from this site in text (*.txt) format in the following languages.
Danish Dutch English Finnish French
German Italian Portuguese Spanish Swedish

Figure 3.12   Wherever you are thinking of going, this checklist can help you identify problems and solutions

Universities' disability statements

The Disability Discrimination Act 1995 requires institutions funded by the higher education funding councils in the UK to publish disability statements every three years. These statements look at:

- current policy;
- current provision;
- future activities and policy development.

It's an easy way to compare institutions in relation to your particular need. Each university makes their statement available on the Web and the CANDO site gives access to all of them.

Choosing the Right Place

The way in which a university presents its disability statement and related pages on the Web can be a good indication of how much thought they've given to the issues. The Open University for example, has a facility for you to download the statement in Real Audio as well as document format.

Choice of subject and course type

Your disability or special need may mean that some courses are not suitable. You are probably the best judge of what you can do, but be realistic. Web resources can help you investigate all the additional concerns you may have, such as the following:

- Are teaching and other buildings accessible?
- Are the methods of teaching and assessment flexible?
- What extra help would be available for work placements on a sandwich course?
- What experience does the university department have of providing support for students with special needs?
- Are electronic study aids available?
- Does the career area the course leads to have a positive attitude towards disability?

Entry requirements

If disability has affected your education, your exam results may not be an accurate reflection of your capabilities. Universities will take account of this, but need to satisfy themselves that you have the academic potential to cope with the course.

The location and physical environment

If you have good support at home, you may wish to remain there while you study. On the other hand, leaving home to study in a new location could give you independence if it is coupled with support. Additional factors to consider in your choice of institution are the following:

- Is suitable accommodation offered?

- Is medical help readily available?
- Are non-teaching rooms and areas, such as the students union, canteen and sports facilities, accessible?
- Are parking facilities available?

The Open University (OU)

Many students find the flexibility offered by the Open University a real bonus. Study is part time and done from home, so can be fitted around other commitments or constraints. The OU has developed comprehensive and innovative support systems for disabled students, including:

- alternative media for course materials, such as audio cassette versions of printed course material and subtitled videos;
- free equipment loan schemes, such as talking scientific calculators;
- communication support at tutorials and residential schools;
- a wide range of facilities for examinations and other forms of course assessment.

The main disadvantage to studying with the OU is that, because it is part time, you are not eligible for the Disabled Students Allowance (see Chapter 5).

Higher education and dyslexia

It is estimated that 2 per cent of undergraduates are dyslexic. Universities recognize that these students have different learning styles and are developing policies to support them. However, such provision is patchy and varied. An individual university's Web site will give you an overview of its attitude to dyslexia. Start with the disability statement. This gives the number of current students assessed as dyslexic and details of the support available. The kind of support given can include:

- specialist assessment – students may be asked to pay for this;

- help with applying for a Disabled Students Allowance (see Chapter 5);
- access to software and other equipment designed for dyslexic students;
- advice on buying or renting specialist equipment;
- help with arranging specialist personal support, such as proofreaders and note-takers;
- study skills and exam preparation for dyslexic students.

You should also look for detailed information relating to dyslexia and study. The University of Ulster, for example, has excellent pages that include practical suggestions on learning strategies for lecturers and students (see Figure 3.13).

If you have a disability, it's essential that you visit the institution and check that the reality matches your understanding and expectations. You should see how accessible it is for you and get a sense of the atmosphere. Try to meet other disabled students while you're there and hear about their experiences. Visits should be arranged as early as possible. In some cases,

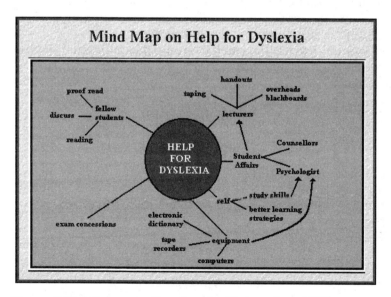

Figure 3.13 Support offered at the University of Ulster. Some dyslexic students find information presented in this way easier to understand

universities will need to modify buildings to accommodate your needs and this takes time.

Your first point of contact will be the disability office. It offers support to prospective and current students with a special need. Its services include:

- an opportunity to discuss learning and support require-ments before or during a course;
- arranging visits to the university to assess the suitability of facilities;
- information about university procedures and policies, such as admissions and equal opportunities;
- referrals to agencies that can carry out assessments for specialist equipment;
- arrangement of dyslexia assessments;
- support and assistance with applying for the Disabled Students Allowance;
- arrangement of modified assessment and examination procedures;
- information about specialist equipment in the university;
- coordination of personal communication support, such as note-takers, sign language interpreters;
- guidance to teaching staff to ensure that individual student requirements are met.

PARTNERSHIPS

Academic

The links universities have developed with overseas institu-tions are an important consideration. The international oppor-tunities a course offers can have enormous implications for future job prospects, as well as being exciting in themselves. There is more on this in Chapter 6.

Employer

Universities develop links with employers. This can be because:

- they have expertise in relation to a particular industry;
- senior staff in the company are former students;
- they are in the same locality.

Universities will feature these links on their departmental Web sites. Examples include The University of Southampton and The Royal Navy; The University of Loughborough and British Aerospace. Such relationships can mean that those employers sponsor students or have an input into course content or teaching.

STUDENT LIFE

You could be forgiven for thinking that student life is all about study, jobs and money. They are major concerns but there are also good social reasons for going to university. Most students have a wonderful time there. To ensure that you do, check what's on offer to keep you cheerful, sane and relaxed.

Societies and social events

If you have an interest you want to pursue or a new activity you'd like to take up, you'll find masses to choose from. You don't have to wait till you get there to see what's on offer. Visit the societies' and students' union sites (see Figure 3.14) to get details of forthcoming events and attractions. It could just tip the balance between one university and another for you!

The student newspaper

Most universities have a student newspaper with an online version. Looking at this will reassure you that student life is not all hard work and give you a glimpse into the other bits. If you're a budding journalist or writer, get involved with it at an early stage.

If this sounds a wee bit daunting, fear not, for there is an organisation entirely devoted to helping you get the most out of your time at Queen's. The Students' Union is administered by students for students and our aim is to provide good quality service and representation to all our members (you automatically become a member when you enrol as a student).

The most obvious, and indeed popular, of our service areas is commercial services. Our two bars offer the cheapest beer in Belfast and we provide a varied programme of entertainment. We also run a shop which caters for all your needs at very competitive prices.

Unfortunately these days student life is certainly not all beer and skittles – financial problems, academic difficulties, problems with accommodation and personal issues can all have a negative impact on students. To help alleviate this we play an important role in the University's welfare and support network.

University gives you a great chance to indulge in your interests and develop new ones. We have 55 sporting clubs and almost 100 non-sporting. We provide training to those who take on positions of responsibility in clubs and societies or in other areas of student life. Graduates with proof of this kind of personal development are much sought after by employers, so taking part can be more than just a good laugh. Most students tend to pack a lot of living into an all too brief period at University. At the Students' Union we're here to help with the difficulites and we're here to share the celebrations too.

Figure 3.14   The students' union offers a range of services and facilities

The surrounding area

University Web sites include links that help you explore the surroundings (see Figure 3.15). Reading the local paper is a good way of getting a feel for an area. Many regional papers now have on-line versions too. Home students don't normally bother to look at the sections for international students, but the information universities gather for this group can also be enlightening for students moving from one part of the UK to another (see Chapter 8).

Yorkshire

- City of York Council

- Digital Yorkshire

- Yorkshire and Humberside Arts

- Yorkshire and Humberside Development Agency

- Yorkshire Evening Press

- Yorkshire Tourist Board `Updated`

- Yorkshire WWWeb Guide

- Yorkshire and Humberside Universities Association Information Server

- YorkshireNet

Figure 3.15 The University of York has selected Web sites to help you explore life outside the university

OPEN DAYS

Virtual visits are an effective way of making a first assessment of a place but no substitute for the real thing. What's on a university's Web site has been selected with the aim of promoting it. If you're seriously considering a place, you should go and see it for yourself (see Figure 3.16). University Web sites will have up-to-date information on open days (see Figure A.11). If you can't make one of the organized ones, contact the department to check if an individual visit can be arranged. Some universities combine interviews with open days.

Complete the checklist on page 73 for each university you are considering. Your information will mainly come from your chosen university's Web site. Where resources from other chapters need to be used, reference is made to them.

University of Bath Open Days

Which of these questions are important to you?

Listed below are suggested questions which you may wish to ask during your visit to University of Bath

- 'I am doing A levels/BTEC ND/GNVQ (Adv) in … subjects. Which degrees particularly relate to these qualifications, given my particular interest in …'
- How will I be assessed on the course – by continuous assessment or by exams? How often will exams take place?
- How much time will I spend in lectures, in private study, in tutorials, in laboratory work etc.?
- For sandwich courses – does the department organise work placements or is the student expected to arrange them?
- Are sandwich courses better than the shorter course?
- Do you interview all applicants? What are they asked at interview?
- What is the average intake of students each year, and proportion of women to men?
- Is taking a 'year out' acceptable or encouraged? if so, is a specific experience sought?
- How flexible is the course? Is there scope for pursuing interests or even changing subjects?
- What careers are open to me after graduating in this subject?
- What is the standard and cost of accommodation generally?
- For students who 'live out', is there enough reasonable accommodation available nearby?
- Is public transport available, eg, from Bath? What does it cost?
- Are computer facilities available for undergraduate use?
- What sports activities are available? Are they free?
- Do you have drama and music facilities?
- How much extra money will I need to have?
- What's the difference between Semesters and Terms? How will it affect my studies?
- The University of Bath runs modular courses – what does this mean for me as a student?

Figure 3.16 Before visiting a university, you should have an idea of what you need to find out

CHECKLIST 3: COMPARING UNIVERSITIES

University:

Course:

Open days:

Actual entry requirements:

Ratio of applicants to places:

Ratio of staff to students:

Relevant staff details:

Teaching methods:

Assessment methods:
(Exams, practical assessments, continuous assessment, placement)

Course structure:

Additional professional qualifications offered:

Assessment report highlights:
(See also Chapter 4)

Employer links:
(See also Chapter 5)

International opportunities:
(See also Chapter 6)

Availability and cost of accommodation:

Cost of living:
(See also Chapter 8)

Financial incentives:
(See also Chapter 5)

Learning resources:
Highlights:

Costs?

Careers service highlights:

Student destinations:

Societies and events I'd enjoy:

What it's like to live in:
(See also Chapter 8)

Why this course is in my final selection:

Other considerations:

SITES WORTH SEEING

Note: For links to all universities, see under Sites worth seeing in Chapter 2.

Scotland

Scottish Law Society

http://www.lawscot.org.uk
Information is given on training for, and working in, the Scottish legal system.

The Scottish Office

http://www.hmis.scotoff.gov.uk
The 'Education and training in Scotland' section provides an authoritative guide to all aspects of education in the country. There is an overview of higher education provision and links to all Scottish higher education institutions.

General Teaching Council for Scotland

http://www.gtcs.org.uk
Information on registration requirements for teaching in Scotland can be found here (see Figure 3.5).

Student life

Note: See also sites listed under Other considerations in Chapter 8.

There are lots of sites competing to be the place for students. The selection that follows offers information and entertainment that gives real insight into student life:

http://www.redmole.co.uk
http://www.studentuk.com
http://www.studentzone.org.uk

National Union of Students (NUS)

http://www.nus.org.uk
The NUS represents student interests. Its site has information on all issues and details of how to help influence policy. There's a link to all student newspapers with on-line versions.

Special concerns

Association for Higher Education Access and Disability (AHEAD)

http://www.ahead.ie

This site has information for students in both Northern Ireland and the Republic on all matters related to disability and higher education.

CANDO

http://cando.lancs.ac.uk

This is a national Internet service that assists disabled students and graduates in preparing for and finding employment. It includes a listing of all universities' disability statements, information on employment service schemes, advice about disabled people's job rights, vacancy listings, as well as a mailing list, disability-careers-forum.

Disability Now

http://www.disabilitynow.org.uk

This is the newspaper for people with an interest in disabilities.

The Dyslexia Archive

http://www.hensa.ac.uk/dyslexia.html

This is a collection of material covering all aspects of dyslexia. It includes information on dyslexia support at university and the Disabled Student's Allowance.

The Dyslexia Institute

http://www.dyslexia-inst.org.uk

The Institute aims to help dyslexic children and adults benefit fully from education. It can help with assessments, teaching and give advice on obtaining funding.

Knowledge Media Institute

http://met.open.ac.uk

The Institute is part of the Open University and focuses on applications in multimedia and enabling technologies. This site maintains a comprehensive list of disability-related Internet links.

sites worth seeing

Related mailing lists

The following can all can be subscribed to via Mailbase — see Appendix:

- deaflink, for deaf undergraduates and their support staff;
- ment-assist, Mental Health Issues in Higher Education;
- disability-careers-forum, discusses issues related to employment for people with disabilities.

University Assessments

This chapter addresses the vexed question of what makes a 'good' university and shows how information freely available on the Internet can provide specific and almost objective answers.

- Quality assessment of higher education
- Initial teacher training assessments
- Research assessment exercise
- *The Times'* university league tables
- Employer assessments
- Professional bodies' assessments
- Student assessments
- Sites worth seeing

The most commonly asked question about higher education choice is 'Which is the best university?' It's easy to find opinions on the quality of degrees, but, even at its most scientific, measuring and comparing educational experiences is inexact, open to criticism and varied interpretation. One problem is that you are looking back at what happened to previous students. All the criteria judged can alter as a result of changes in funding or staff.

The Internet gives you access to the best comparative information from a range of formal and informal sources. It allows

---

The results are in!

Over the last nine months, over 12 000 students from all over the country have been giving us their verdicts on their own universities. Never mind the official rankings, or the guides that have been appearing in the newspapers, here's the rating that really matters - a true reflection of student satisfaction. If you didn't vote, it's too late (but we'll start again in September): here's the Alternative University Rankings 1997-8.

Congratulations to Durham, who finished top of the heap overall, and had best accommodation and architecture. Lancaster has the best totty of both sexes. and tops several other categories, but was let down by appalling accommodation and architecture. Loughborough have the best sporting facilities and Leeds is the place to go for a great night out. Welsh colleges scored quite highly, but overall it is a triumph for the North!

For a more detailed look at the results, you can either check out the <u>overall ratings</u> or you can look at the ratings in each category:

- <u>Accommodation</u>
- <u>Quality of teaching</u>
- <u>Services provided by the union</u>
- <u>Sporting facilities</u>
- <u>Attractiveness of males</u>
- <u>Attractiveness of females</u>

- <u>Access to computer facilities</u>
- <u>Freshers' Week</u>
- <u>Relationship with locals</u>
- <u>Architecture</u>
- <u>Nightlife</u>
- <u>Careers Advice</u>

Figure 4.1 Red Mole gives an interesting insight into what students think of their universities

you to look at surveys and studies and extract relevant information. Each way of comparing universities has flaws, so assessment findings should not be the sole basis of your choice of course, but, rather, one factor among all the others covered in this book.

QUALITY ASSESSMENT OF HIGHER EDUCATION

In the United Kingdom, the quality of higher education provision is assessed by three bodies – one for England and Northern Ireland, one for Scotland and one for Wales. All aim to:

- ensure that education is of an acceptable quality;
- provide publicly accessible information;
- encourage improvements.

Methods of grading vary from council to council, but these are explained on their Web sites. Assessments measure 'the extent to which each subject provider is successful in achieving their set aims and objectives'. As each institution is autonomous and determines its own aims and objectives, it is not necessarily valid to compare one institution with another based on these reports. They provide a snapshot in time of how a place is doing in relation to targets it has set itself.

The Higher Education Funding Council for England (HEFCE)

The HEFCE covers the 140 institutions of higher education and 75 further education colleges in England and Northern Ireland that offer degree-level study. Due to the quantity of courses, not all subjects have been covered yet. HEFCE's Web site gives a detailed timetable for current and projected assessments.

Concise reports on assessed courses and institutions are available on the site. These are based on observation of all the teaching and learning activities; analysis of the institutions self-assessment and statistical indicators, such as exam results, student destinations and drop-out rates. In the latest reports, the following areas are assessed:

- curriculum design, content and organization;
- teaching, learning and assessment;
- student progression and achievement;
- student support and guidance;
- learning resources;
- quality assurance and enhancement.

Each is graded on a four-point scale, with 4 being excellent and 1 representing unsatisfactory provision. The maximum potential score for any course is therefore 24 points. Those departments or courses at, or near, to this figure feature it prominently in their publicity material.

The earliest assessments – made between 1993 and 1995 – were based on a three-point scale — excellent, satisfactory and unsatisfactory. The process is ongoing, with some subjects scheduled for their first assessment in 2001. Each report clearly states when the assessment was carried out and it is important to take that into account. Major changes for better or worse may have taken place in the intervening years. Reports give detailed information and grading for each of the assessed areas, a summary of the course's strong points and issues that need to be addressed. Students should check for changes made in response to weaknesses previously identified.

Reports can be viewed by subject or institution. Looking at an overview of an institution's grading is good for dispelling prejudices and proves the point that there is no such thing as a good or bad university. All have a mixture of strengths and weaknesses.

Reports of a Quality Assessment in History

Reports by Institution

- University of Aberdeen   HIGHLY SATISFACTORY
- University of Dundee   HIGHLY SATISFACTORY
- University of Edinburgh   EXCELLENT
- University of Glasgow   HIGHLY SATISFACTORY
- University of St Andrews   EXCELLENT
- University of Stirling   HIGHLY SATISFACTORY
- University of Strathclyde   HIGHLY SATISFACTORY
- The text of all 7 reports may be downloaded as one Word 6 document (288k) by clicking **here**

Figure 4.2 For each subject a report for all institutions assessed can be downloaded

The Scottish Higher Education Funding Council (SHEFC)

Covers all institutions providing higher education in Scotland. Assessments are undertaken on a six-year rolling programme. The first cycle of assessments was completed in the academic year 1997–98.

Assessment is on a four-point scale:

- excellent – satisfactory in all and outstanding in most aspects;

- highly satisfactory – satisfactory in all aspects and with areas of particular strength;
- satisfactory – satisfactory in most aspects; overall strengths outweigh weaknesses;
- unsatisfactory – unsatisfactory in several aspects; overall weaknesses outweigh strengths.

Published reports are distributed to each school and careers office in Scotland and made available on the SHEFC's Web site (see Figure 4.2).

The Higher Education Funding Council for Wales (HEFCW)

The HEFCW covers provision at all institutions offering higher education courses in Wales. Assessments were carried out between 1993 and 1997. This was on a three-point scale, but all provision was judged to be either satisfactory or excellent. The Web site gives an overview of assessment grades listed by institution and subject. There are plans to make full reports available on the Web.

INITIAL TEACHER TRAINING ASSESSMENTS

The Teacher Training Agency published the first set of performance profiles for initial teacher training (ITT) in England in September 1998, and plans to update these annually. The profiles give detailed information on three areas:

- characteristics and entry qualifications of first-year trainees;
- percentage of the previous year's finalists being awarded qualified teacher status, and their employment status in March after graduation;
- information from OFSTED inspections of ITT provision.

The information is detailed and complicated. The whole set of profiles can be downloaded from the Web (see Figure 4.3) or else you can print/store specific pages from the site.

St Martin's College

<u>Profile 1A</u>: First year trainees on ITT courses in 1996/97 – Characteristics

<u>Profile 1B</u>: First year trainees on ITT courses in 1996/97 – Characteristics

<u>Profile 2A</u>: First year trainees on ITT courses in 1996/97 – Entry qualification – Undergraduate

<u>Profile 2A</u>: First year trainees on ITT courses in 1996/97 – Entry qualification – Postgraduate

<u>Profile 2B</u>: Final year trainees on ITT courses in 1996/97 – Entry qualifications – Undergraduate

<u>Profile 2B</u>: Final year trainees on ITT courses in 1996/97 – Entry qualifications – Postgraduate

<u>Profile 3</u>: Final year trainees on ITT courses in 1996/97 – Percentage awarded QTS in 1997 – Undergraduate

<u>Profile 4</u>: Final year trainees awarded QTS in 1996/97 – Employment status on 2 March 1998 – Undergraduate

<u>Profile 4</u>: Final year trainees awarded QTS in 1996/97 – Employment status on 2 March 1998 – Postgraduate

<u>Profile 5A</u>: OFSTED primary inspection (1994–96) grades awarded

<u>Profile 5B</u>: OFSTED primary inspection (1996/97) grades awarded

<u>Profile 6</u>: OFSTED secondary subject inspection (1996/97) grades awarded

---

Figure 4.3 The Web-based information is easier to navigate through than the paper version

Teacher training provision in Scotland is assessed by the SHEFC in the same way as other degree subjects.

RESEARCH ASSESSMENT EXERCISE

The funding councils also carry out a research assessment exercise every five years. This covers all subjects, and findings are used as a basis for allocating future research grants. Ratings are on a scale from 5*, denoting international excellence, to 1, which shows an absence of excellence (see Figure 4.4).

Individual departments with high research ratings will highlight this in the prospectus pages. The relevance postgraduate research has to undergraduates is that outstanding research means outstanding staff and facilities, which has a knock-on effect for all teaching in a department. However, there is not always a correlation between research and teaching. The University of Portsmouth's French department, for example, attained 23 points in its HEFCE assessment, but only a 3b for research.

This discrepancy is more noticeable amongst the new universities. Research rankings favour the older universities and the system is self-perpetuating. The better an institution's research, the more likely it is to secure funding for further research and so rank highly in future. Because of this, it is the area of assessment that raises the most controversy. The last research assessment exercise was conducted in 1996 and the next one will be carried out in 2001.

Psychology

Psychology Panel

Institution	1996 Rating
University of Birmingham	4
Birkbeck College	5
Bolton Institute of HE	2
University of Bristol	5
Brunel University	3a
University of Cambridge	5*
University of Central Lancashire	3b
City University	4
Coventry University	2
De Montfort University	2
University of Derby	2

Figure 4.4   A summary of research assessment exercise ratings by subject and institution can be seen on the funding councils' Web sites

THE TIMES' UNIVERSITY LEAGUE TABLES

Every year, around the middle of May, *The Times* publishes league tables of UK universities and supplements these with a series of related articles and analyses. These are also available on its Web site. The tables give an overview of how universities perform in a range of fields. In 1998, 96 UK universities were included. The final rankings are arrived at by giving a score out of 100 to 8 areas:

- teaching assessment;
- research assessment;
- entry standards;
- staff–student ratios;
- library and computer spending;
- spending on facilities, such as careers and accommodation services;
- the number of First Class and Upper Second degrees;
- graduate destinations.

The areas are reviewed each year to reflect changes in higher education, so, for example, computer spending was added in 1998 to reflect its growing importance. It's essential to remember that these rankings relate to the whole university, but what is relevant to an individual is how their course performs. Library and computing spending will affect all students, but staff to student ratios are averaged across the whole university and there may be differences between departments.

Comparative assessments always place older universities above newer ones. If you look at the top ten 'new' universities you will see that they were a good way down in the overall rankings (see Table 1.2). The reasons for this are the subject of continuing discussion and disagreement, aired by *The Times* alongside the league tables.

Overall rankings need to be looked at in relation to their component criteria. For example, only two universities scored 100 for student destinations – Cambridge and Surrey. In the overall ratings, however, Cambridge came first and Surrey 39th. In facilities spending, Oxford, with an overall rating of second, came 44th.

How universities compare for any one individual depends on what is important to them. *The Times'* league tables give you a quick way to compare what universities provide. The Internet enables you to delve deeper into each of the criteria and look at the source material.

It's inevitable that such information will have an influence on your perceptions of courses and institutions. Alongside that, bear in mind that the best university for you is the one that meets all your needs. Important criteria are that you will:

- be offered a place;
- be able to cope with the study there;
- enjoy all the other aspects of being at that university.

If you are predicted high grades, you may have a choice from among those consistently at the top of all league tables. If you are closer to the average, then you may not. Entry grades are not entirely a reflection of academic rigour or quality, but more accurately of popularity. In many cases, a course or university is popular because it is regarded as offering a high-quality student experience.

EMPLOYER ASSESSMENTS

For many students, the most important measure of a course is the job opportunities it will open up. Prospective students want to know how employers will rate their course. Once again, Web-based information can help you investigate this.

Some employers have a tradition of recruiting students from certain universities. This does not mean that they will exclude applicants from other universities, but if they repeatedly recruit people from a particular course, that is a resounding vote of confidence in it. Courses and departments with such links use their Web sites to show who is actively recruiting at their university. If there's a particular employer you're interested in, you could e-mail its graduate recruitment department and ask if the company has a preference for a university or course. Use a search engine (see Appendix) or one of the directories at the end of this chapter to find employer Web sites and contact details.

Even when an employer does not target a specific university for recruitment, many departmental or careers service Web sites make a point of showing the successes of former students. The University of East Anglia, for example, has a scheme that puts current students in contact with former ones to research career options (see Figure 3.7).

Employers providing sponsorships will often stipulate courses they approve of. In some cases, rather than naming specific courses, they look for students on courses accredited by the relevant professional body. There is information on this in Chapter 5.

Accredited Degree Courses

The IEE accredits first degree course in electrical, electronic, manufacturing and computer based systems engineering. Accredited courses have been subjected to rigorous scrutiny, during which a great many features have been considered. The main ones are:

- quality of students (entry standards, motivation etc.)
- quality of staff (qualifications, research, publications)
- evidence of quality assurance procedures
- aims and philosophy of of the course
- structure and content of the course (balanced up-to-date curriculum, inclusion of non-technical subjects and current industrial practices)
- inclusion of design (CADCAM, reliability, maintainability, marketability, etc.)
- inclusion of engineering applications through case studies and projects
- assessment (level and style of examinations, role of projects, communications skills, etc.)
- industrial contact (industrial visits/lectures, liaison)
- resources (library, computing, laboratories, staff support)

IEE accredited courses are therefore of a high quality and will inculcate in graduates a professional engineering ethos appropriate to the demands of the profession. Continuing post-graduate education and training, however, will be required to keep a professional engineer abreast of the fast changing technology of the profession.

The list of addredited UK degree courses is updated regularly. This is a Microsoft Word 6.0 document.

Figure 4.5 Accreditation by a professional body is awarded after rigorous assessment

PROFESSIONAL BODIES' ASSESSMENTS

In certain subjects – such as engineering, architecture and psychology – professional bodies accredit courses (see Figure 4.5). For some professions, completion of an approved degree course is a prerequisite for professional training. Details of how to find professional bodies' Web sites are given in Chapter 2.

STUDENT ASSESSMENTS

Many students rely on hearsay, with their final choice being influenced as much by what their friends say, which football team they support or where their current loved one is going. The Web allows you to have access to more anecdotal and unreliable information than was ever possible before!

As well as the intriguing Red Mole findings (see Figures 4.1 and 4.6), you can access higher education-related chat lines, message boards and newsgroups to find out what other students are saying about the place you're thinking of going to. After all, university is not just about studying and debt.

Some Comments about the
Alternative University Ratings

'If this survey is to be believed, for my entire life I have been fooled into thinking that Oxford was academia's principle – when really that honour belonged to the University of East London.'
Tutor, Corpus Christi College, Oxford

'People here come from a higher class of society – the good breeding produces fitter women.'
Economics Student, Durham

'I chose to come here because of the girl on a bicycle on the front of the prospectus. I didn't care about the course.'
History Student, Lancaster

Figure 4.6   Red Mole's findings arouse controversy just like all the other league tables

Use the checklist below to decide which aspects of assessments and league tables are important to you.

CHECKLIST 4: ASSESSMENTS
Web resources to use
University:
Course:
How did it score in the funding council assessment? *Funding council sites*
When was the assessment carried out? *Funding council sites*
What were its strong points? *Funding council sites*
What were its weak points? *Funding council sites*
Any major changes since the assessment? *University Web sites*
How did the whole university fare? *Funding council sites*

What research grade did the department achieve? Is there a discrepancy between the research and teaching assessments?
Funding council sites

How does my subject at this university compare with other universities?
Funding council sites

Which of *The Times'* criteria are important to me?
The Times' Good University Guide

Any evidence of what employers think of this course? Which companies regularly recruit students from it?
Careers service pages
Employers' sites
Graduate recruitment and careers information sites

Any professional recognition included?
Professional bodies' sites
University Web site

What do students say about the university and the course?
Red Mole
Student newspapers
Student UK
Studentzone
Discussion/chat forums
Newsgroups

—————— SITES WORTH SEEING ——————

The Quality Assurance Agency for Higher Education (QAA)
http://www.niss.ac.uk/education/qaa
The QAA promotes improvement in quality and provides public information about higher education. It is currently working towards implementing the recommendations in the Dearing and Garrick reports. You can keep up to date with developments by visiting this Web site.

Funding councils

Higher Education Funding Council for England (HEFCE)
http://www.hefce.ac.uk
HEFCE is planning a 'higher education mall' for the Internet. This should be available from 2000, and aims to provide access to sites students need when researching options. Details of progress can be found in the news and events section of the site.

Higher Education Funding Council for Wales (HEFCW).
http://www.wfc.ac.uk/hefcw/index.html

Research assessment exercise
http://www.niss.ac.uk/education/hefc/rae96/

Scottish Higher Education Funding Council (SHEFC)
http://www.shefc.ac.uk/shefc/welcome.htm

Teacher Training Agency
http://www.teach-tta.gov.uk/itt.htm

Other assessments

The Alternative University Ratings Table
http://www.redmole.co.uk
Compiled by students for students. A refreshingly different look at what matters (see Figures 4.1 and 4.6).

The Times

http://www.times.co.uk

You need to complete a registration document to access material on this site. The university league tables are in the 'Education guides' section of 'Resources'.

Employer directories

For the UK try:

The Biz

http://www.thebiz.co.uk

or:

UK Business Net

http://www.ukbusinessnet.com

Both provide basic company information, hypertext links to companies that have Web sites and contact information for those that don't.

For US and global companies, look at:

Hoover's Corporate Web Sites

http://www.hoovers.com

Hoover's has links to Web sites for more than 5000 of the world's largest companies.

sites worth seeing

Student Finance

Use the Web to gain accurate and up-to-date information on the cost of higher education and find sources of additional income that can help ease the potential poverty of being a student.

- Fees and loans
- National Health Service bursaries
- Special concerns
- Other sources of money
- Bursaries, prizes and scholarships
- Sponsorship
- Sandwich courses
- Part-time and vacation work
- Help with budgeting
- Student banking
- Sites worth seeing

FEES AND LOANS

What will it cost?

The student funding system in the UK is complicated and subject to change. Generalizations about financial entitlements for students are fraught with problems – even material printed by government departments dates quickly. The

---

STUDENT AWARDS AGENCY FOR SCOTLAND (SAAS)
Welcome to the SAAS Undergraduate Homepage.

Your student grand/loan questions answered
OUR REMIT, AIMS AND PROCESSING STATISTICS
FREQUENTLY ASKED QUETIONS
WHAT COURSES DO WE ASSIST?
ARE YOU ELIGIBLE FOR SUPPORT
HEALTH PROFESSION STUDENTS
1. Arrangements for Degree courses in Nursing, Midwifery and the Professions Allied to Medicine (PAMS)
2. Arrangements for Medical and Dental students
STUDENTS FROM EUROPEAN MEMBER STATES
STUDENTS FROM OUTWITH THE UK

Figure 5.1 The DfEE and SAAS Web sites have comprehensive information on financial arrangements for students

departments that govern student funding have regularly updated Web sites and these are the most reliable sources of information (see Figure 5.1). Other organizations use their sites to offer advice and guidance on managing finances and interpreting the regulations.

The basic financial facts at the time of writing are as follows:

- Home students (those normally resident in the UK – a full definition can be found on the DfEE Web site; information for overseas students can be found in Chapter 8) will be asked to pay up to £1025 per academic year towards tuition fees, depending on their own, their parents' or spouse's income. Local education authorities (LEAs) assess applications and decide on entitlement to support for fees. It is expected that this amount will be adjusted annually to take account of inflation.
- All students must apply for an LEA assessment, otherwise they will not be eligible for subsidized fees or student loan.
- Students on health professional degree courses in receipt of an NHS bursary (some students on health professional degree courses may not receive this – see page 98) do not pay tuition fees and are eligible for a means-tested bursary and student loans.

- Students on diploma courses in nursing and midwifery do not pay tuition fees and are eligible for a non-means-tested bursary and student loan.
- Students who normally live in Scotland will not have to pay fees for the final year if the same course could be done in a shorter time elsewhere in the UK.
- No university should charge 'top-up' fees in addition to the tuition fee.
- Some courses may require compulsory payment of additional charges – for example, field trips, special equipment or materials that are necessary for the course.
- The biggest expenditure for most students is day-to-day living costs. From 1999, there will no longer be grant aid towards these, but all full-time students will be eligible for a loan.

Loans available to students

The Student Loan Company administers the national scheme that makes a mortgage-style loan available to eligible students. About a quarter of the total loan available will be means-tested. All students will be entitled to the remaining three quarters.

A discretionary hardship loan of between £100 and £250 is available to students in financial hardship, provided they have already applied for their maximum student loan. It is targeted at students who might otherwise have to abandon their course. Interest-free overdrafts from banks are described later in the chapter.

The Department for Education and Employment (DfEE) will be carrying out a review of funding arrangements to simplify, update and remove anomalies. It does not intend to implement any changes in 1999/2000, but some are possible for 2000/2001. The DfEE and Student Loan Company Web sites provide the factual information. If you want to look at analyses of what these changes mean for students, look at the NUS Web site.

The Access Fund

The government allocates a sum of money known as the Access Fund to every higher and further education institution in the UK. It provides additional funds for students suffering unusual financial hardship. Institutions have criteria for distributing this and details can be found in the finance sections on their Web sites.

Where does the money go?

Everyone has different spending priorities, but accommodation is the largest item for most students. If you go to university and live at home, it will be less of a drain on your finances, but may have detrimental effects on your social life!

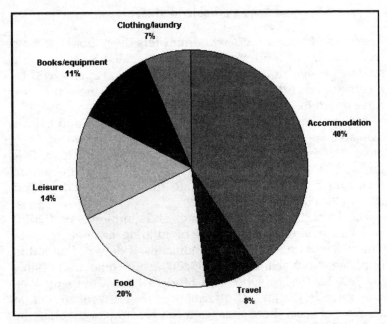

Figure 5.2 Lloyds Bank give a good indication of what uses up your money (excluding fees)

As prices vary considerably between different cities and regions of the UK, you need to look in detail at the costs associated with living in each area. Accommodation costs can easily be found, but other expenditure is more difficult to estimate. A good source of detailed and realistic information is the international students section of a university's Web site.

Expenditure	52 weeks £	38 weeks £
Accommodation Single room on or next to campus, average £41 a week [Note]	2132.00	1558.00
Meals at £7.00 a day, £49.00 a week [Note]	2548.00	1862.00
Books and stationery (inc photocopying) [Note]	400.00	400.00
General living expenses (entertainment, laundry, 'pocket money' etc Total £30 a week [Note]	1560.00	1140.00
TOTAL	**6640.00** (approx.)	**4960.00** (approx.)

Figure 5.3 Cost of living information from the international section of York University's Web site

Entitlement to benefits

Most full-time students are excluded from benefits such as Jobseekers Allowance, Income Support and Housing Benefit. However, these continue to be available to students in vulnerable groups, such as lone parents with children under 16 and students with disabilities.

NATIONAL HEALTH SERVICE BURSARIES

Students accepted on diploma courses in nursing or mid-wifery are eligible for a non-means-tested bursary and do not pay fees. Students with an NHS-funded place on degree courses in physiotherapy, occupational therapy, radiography, orthoptics, dental hygiene, dental therapy, nursing, mid-wifery, speech and language therapy, chiropody, dietetics, prosthetics, and orthotics are eligible for a means-tested bursary. However, some universities may offer extra places on these degree courses that will not be NHS funded.

In order to be sure of filling courses, universities regularly make more offers than there are places available. Some students holding offers will not get the grades, while others may drop out. If a university miscalculates and has more students than places after exam results are published, they have to honour offers to students who meet the conditions stated. However, any places additional to NHS requirements will not be funded, and students taking those places will not receive a bursary. The advice from UCAS to students applying for these courses is that they should be:

> aware that they are unlikely to know with any certainty whether they will receive NHS funding until offers are confirmed towards the end of the application cycle in August. There will be differences in the way that individual institutions deal with offers for NHS-funded courses. Therefore at the time they receive an offer students should obtain as much information as possible from the institution about how their place will be funded.

A free booklet on NHS financial support for students can be obtained from:

NHSB, Department of Health, PO Box 410, Wetherby LS23 7LN

SPECIAL CONCERNS

All the sources of funding described in this chapter are available to disabled students. However, students with special needs may qualify for extra financial help.

Disabled Students' Allowance (DSA)

This is a non-means-tested allowance paid by LEAs to students who can prove they have a disability or medical condition that affects their study. DSAs help pay for extra costs incurred because of your disability, such as items of specialist equipment and a non-medical personal helper.

You can apply for a DSA if you are attending a full-time or sandwich course at a publicly funded UK university or college, leading to a:

- first degree or comparable qualification;
- Diploma of Higher Education (DipHE);
- Higher National Diploma (HND);
- initial teacher training (ITT) qualification.

Your LEA cannot meet the costs of diagnosing your disability to establish your eligibility for a DSA. Check what evidence it will require before you submit your application. For example, if you are dyslexic, your LEA needs evidence of your dyslexia from either:

- a qualified psychologist experienced in working with dyslexic adults;
- someone with a qualification from a professional training course involving the assessment of adults with dyslexia.

Up-to-date information on the allowance can be found in the DfEE publication *Bridging the Gap*, which is available on its Web site. There is a free and confidential benefits enquiry line (0800 88 22 00) for people with disabilities and their carers (minicom users can dial 0800 24 33 55).

OTHER SOURCES OF MONEY

Student hardship has been a reality for a long time. The new arrangements place more of the burden on students and their families. Students now have to be more enterprising in order to avoid serious debt. Many employers, professional bodies and charities are responding to the new situation with support schemes. These can be sponsorships, golden hellos or paid vacation work.

Additional funds can come from a diverse range of sources and are often awarded on a competitive basis. Finding what's available and doing the research to make a strong application is time-consuming. The Internet can make searching for relevant information easier.

BURSARIES, PRIZES AND SCHOLARSHIPS

These may be offered by universities and professional organizations. There is no central point of information and examples are included here to highlight what's on offer. An efficient way to find information on the bursaries and scholarships of an organization is to use their sites search facility. As financial incentives for students become more of a feature of higher education, this is an area that will grow and develop.

University bursaries

There are many scholarship schemes for home students. Examples include:

- organ scholarships for most Oxford colleges;
- choral scholarship at Durham;
- hotel and catering management bursary at Dundee;
- economics bursary at Hull;
- John Lennon memorial scholarship at Liverpool;
- sport at Sheffield;
- Royal and Ancient Golf Club bursaries in Scotland and Northern Ireland;
- *Voice* scholarship for British Afro-Caribbean students at Warwick.

Amounts vary but can make a welcome contribution to other funds. Having succeeded in competing for a scholarship looks good on a CV. Some universities have a scholarships officer who can give advice on scholarship opportunities and applications.

Bursary awards announced for local students

Sixteen people in the Humbeside area have won student 'bursary'
scholarships from the University as a reward for excellence and achievement,
intended to encourage more people in the region to take advantage of Higher
Education.

The scholarship winners include several mature students who have overcome
great personal difficulties or made a considerable sacrifice to continue their
studies, and others who show promise of outstanding academic achievement
across a range of disciplines.

They will each receive £500 a year from the University, subject to progress in
their studies, for the duration of their courses.

Among the bursary winners is 58 year old Mary West from Bransholme in
Hull. Mature student John Bell of Hull, has also returned to full-time
education after 23 years to take his BA in Philosophy. Elizabeth Blamires
from Saxby-All-Saints, near Brigg had to overcome dyslexia to get to
university, while Tony Nicholson of Grimsby courageously gave up full-time
employment to gain qualifications in the hope of improving his career
prospects.

Figure 5.4   Hull University encourages wider participation
through bursaries for local students

Professional bodies' bursaries

Many professional bodies offer financial incentives for
degrees they approve. This is particularly true of engineering
where there is a drive to attract more students. The Institute of
Materials, for example, offers a bursary of £1000 to students
with good grades as an incentive to apply for degrees accredited by them. Use the sites in Chapter 2 to investigate what the
professional body concerned with your area of study offers.

Educational charities

Eligibility is often related to where you were born, live, your
parents' occupation, subject or personal circumstances. Searching through directories can be time-consuming, but some of
this information is now available on the Web (see Figure 5.11).
They rarely involve large amounts, but can be good for
mature students, as a common thread is self-improvement for
individuals outside the established school system.

If you have real worries about your financial situation, it's worth contacting the university before you decide that you can't afford to study. They may know of sources of funding that can help. In some cases, the welfare office at a university will apply to charities on your behalf, but only where all other possibilities have been explored and you can prove substantial hardship through no fault of your own.

SPONSORSHIP

This is probably the most attractive and lucrative option, not only in terms of the cash while studying, but also the way it enhances future employment prospects. Most sponsorship deals give you a valuable insight into an occupational area and an employer without asking for a long-term commitment. The type and amount of sponsorship available fluctuates with the state of the economy and an employer's need to attract staff. Some, like DERA, which offers forty £1000 scholarships each year to maths or engineering students, say 'All we ask is that you act as a good ambassador for DERA and an informal representative of our achievements and career opportunities … We also hope that you will spend some of your vacation time working with us'. A Royal Navy cadetship, on the other hand, pays from £8000 in the first year to over £11,000 in the third year to well-qualified engineering and technology student cadets. Commitment after study is to a one-year commissioning course at Sandhurst, followed by a minimum of five years' service.

Of all employer sponsorships, 60 per cent are for engineering and science, which reflects the relative unpopularity of these subjects. These are also areas with the greatest chance of finding related employment after graduation. Employer support is also commonly available for students of:

- law;
- maths;
- business studies;
- finance;
- technology.

There is a growing trend for employers to offer sponsorship to students in their penultimate or final year (see Figure 5.5). At that point, they are able to see evidence of academic ability at degree level and it's better for many students too, enabling them to make long-term decisions after having studied a subject for some time.

WHAT DIFFERENCE WILL OUR SPONSORSHIP MAKE WHEN YOU ARE A GRAUDATE?

No one can promise you success in securing that all important first job after graduation. But if you gain a Local Government Student Sponsorship you'll be on the way to achieving this. The following features make our sponsorship a guaranteed foundation for your future.

- *A paid project during your summer vacation*
  This will be of at least 5 weeks' duration and offers a minimum training allowance of £120 per week.
- *Further prizes for the best management reports*
  On completion of projects all management reports will be entered into a national competition. Two further prizes of £250 and one of £500 will be awarded to the student producing the best management reports. The overall winner will also be presented with the annual trophy.
- *Insight into the management of a Local Authority*
  You will work within a department under the guidance of a mentor to product a management report in a defined area of work. This will give you an insight into a business which strives to provide a quality, caring and cost effective service to local communities.
- *Enhanced job opportunities*
  The experience provides an enviable addition to your CV which in turn should lead to enhanced job opportunities for next year.

The scheme is open to any full-time higher education student completing their penultimte year of studies.

Figure 5.5 Some schemes are available to graduates of all disciplines

What sponsorship entails

There is no such thing as a standard sponsorship deal, but common features include:

- a bursary – sometimes for each year of your course, sometimes for the final year;
- the opportunity for paid work during vacations;
- a mentoring scheme.

There is usually no obligation to work for the company after graduation. Equally, there is no obligation for your sponsor to employ you, but in practice many do. The Armed Forces are an exception to this. They ask for a return of service and the more money they give you, the longer your commitment will be.

National sponsorship schemes

A hard core of employers who regularly sponsor students are featured in publications such as the annual *Springboard Sponsorship for Students* (Hobsons Publishing). Because these are well advertised, they attract a large number of applicants. You can make a more effective application if you research the employers thoroughly using their Web sites (see Figure 5.6).

Many universities have good links with sponsoring employers. You can find details on departmental Web pages or from industrial liaison officers who may advise on, or arrange, sponsorship.

Hidden sponsorship opportunities

Smaller employers may offer support but not advertise the fact. Many like to support local students rather than making sponsorship available on a national basis. Some look favourably on children of employees. A company may not have thought of helping someone through university until you approach them.

As sponsorships usually give the opportunity for paid vacation work, an employer close to your home has the benefit of keeping accommodation and food costs down during your placement. Many employers will consider, or even favour, applicants who work for them for a year before going to university. This is worthy of serious consideration as it helps you start your studies with a positive bank balance and gives you a sporting chance of keeping it that way!

What is Sponsorship, Pre-University, Industrial and Vacation Training?

This scheme aims to encourage people who really wish to develop a career in electronic engineering, perhaps in Research and Development, Project Engineering or in practical Operational Engineering. A variety of options may be available, depending on individual departments' needs within the BBC.

Sponsorship usually comprises of an annual bursary paid at the start of each term, with summer vacation training periods in the BBC. Some departments may also offer **1 year Pre-University training** which may lead to Sponsorship in following years. Sponsorship is usually for a maximum of 3 years, although 4 years may be possible and is available only to degree level students in Electronic Engineering or similar.

The **Vacation Training Scheme** provides a six-week training period during the summer of each year. The aim is to allow those studying to HND or degree level in Electrical/Electronics Engineering, to gain practical work experience in an engineering area of the BBC. It gives you a real insight into the job of a BBC engineer; it gives us the opportunity to see you in a working environment.

You The Person

We are looking for people who really want to pursue a career in Broadcast Engineering. If you wish to work in the field of Technical Operations such as camera, lighting, sound or videotape, then this scheme is not for you.

We need people who:

a) are logically-minded and good problem solvers
b) have an iinterest in practical skills and hobbies
c) are 'team-people' and work well in a team
d) are motivated to a career in broadcast engineering.

If you already enjoy learning, problem-solving and being involved in a variety of tasks and you want to find out more about engineering in broadcasting ... then training with us may be for you.

Figure 5.6   Information you need to make a convincing sponsorship application can be found on company Web sites

Is sponsorship right for you?

The financial lure of sponsorship is strong and it has many other advantages, including:

- pre-arranged vacation work;
- the opportunity to try out an employer and career area;
- enhanced employment prospects on graduation, often with better starting pay.

There are also disadvantages. Being sponsored reduces your freedom by:

- pushing you into making a career decision at an early stage;
- limiting the courses you can apply for;
- reducing your free time during vacations;
- committing you to a period of service with an employer – particularly the Armed Forces.

Like all other aspects of higher education choice, it's a personal decision. You have to examine whether its right for you at this stage. Don't just do it for the money – you've got to enjoy the study and work it leads to. Ask yourself if this course would interest you if sponsorship wasn't available.

Sponsorship application

This is a fiercely competitive pursuit. There are always far more applicants than funds. Early research and application is advisable. You should work to the same timetable as for your course application (see Chapter 7). Start your research in the first year of sixth form or college. Aim to send applications in the first term of your second year. As many sponsoring employers state a preference for particular courses, you need to research sponsorship opportunities alongside course choices. Your UCAS form needs to be submitted long before you know the outcome of sponsorship applications, so you have to want to go on that course even if you're not successful in getting sponsorship.

The Web enables you to carry out research and compose an impressive application. To do this effectively, you should use the resources listed in Chapter 2, including:

- professional bodies' Web sites;
- related online journals;
- academic mailing lists and discussion groups.

Web sites of employers are also essential reading. They will vary in content, but you should find:

- products and markets;
- annual report;
- press releases;
- employee profiles;
- a statement on the company ethos and aims;
- general recruitment information.

Employers with Web sites expect applicants to use them. Where employers sponsor students, they are making an investment in their future managers and leaders. You need to show you are a worthwhile investment. Sponsors will want to see an ability to use information intelligently and so your application for sponsorship should demonstrate this. You need to:

- judge what characteristics, abilities and aptitudes they are looking for;
- show how you meet them;
- demonstrate your written communication skills in a well-crafted application.

Many employers' Web sites make this very easy – they give you all the clues you need as to what they are looking for (see Figure 5.6).

Vacation and summer placement programmes

These can be a precursor to final year sponsorship, but, in themselves, provide welcome experience and cash. Many are competitive and require the same care in applying as a full sponsorship. There are national schemes, such as Shell Step (see Sites worth seeing at the end of this chapter) and ones with individual companies (see Figure 5.7). Employers often give details of these in their graduate recruitment sections and university careers services advertise schemes. If an employer you're interested in does not offer vacation placements, ask if they would consider it in your case. If you research its business and your suitability for it thoroughly, you can present a strong argument for why it should!

Summer Vacation Scheme

This opportunity is designed for undergraduates in their penultimate year of study who have already decided on a career in Business Assurance or Management Consultancy. The duration of these schemes varies from two to nine weeks depending upon the host office.

You will have the opportunity to work alongside a variety of Ernst & Young staff on a range of client assignments; these will be either in-house or at client premises. The nature of these projects will vary depending on which discipline you choose.

This programme provides you with an excellent insight into the variety that a career with Ernst & Young can offer. You should apply to one of these schemes: Chartered Accountancy, Business Analyst or Management Consultancy depending on your preference (unfortunately allocation to specific business units within each discipline cannot be guaranteed due to the number of places available).

Click here to see details of the schemes and vacancies ...
How to apply for Vacational Opportunities

Figure 5.7 Several employers offer schemes similar to this

SANDWICH COURSES

The structure of sandwich courses varies, but the placement year is usually the penultimate year of study. Placements can be in this country or abroad. Who arranges the placement varies too. In some cases, departments or universities have industrial placement officers who do most of the hard work, although students still have to go through a selection process with the employer. In other cases, the onus for finding a placement is on the student. Its worth checking these details before deciding to apply for a course. See Chapter 2 for information on finding sandwich courses.

PART-TIME AND VACATION WORK

This is probably the easiest option for boosting your finances. Not too long ago, students were discouraged from working in term time as it was felt it adversely affected their studies. Now

The Job Shop

The Job Shop is an employment service that has been set up to assist students and recent graduates in their search for part-time and/or temporary work opportunities.

- If you are a full-time student we recommend that you work no more than 15 hours per week during term time and full-time during the vacation periods.

- Work is available either within the University or with external copanies.

- The average rate of pay is £5.00 per hour.

- No previous work experience is required but commitment and reliability is essential.

- The type of work that the Job Shop deals with is extremely varied and has ranged from clerical, secretarial, computing, manual, sales, marketing, catering, gardening, musical etc.

Figure 5.8 The Job Shop at Leeds Metropolitan University

it's positively encouraged because universities realize that financial worries are a greater threat to academic achievement than working. Many universities make a positive and practical contribution towards student job searching during term time. Anglia Polytechnic University, for example, operates an employment agency for students that finds them work within the university or with external employers. Much of that employment is 'credit rated', which means it's relevant to your studies and counts towards your overall assessment.

Job shops for students are an increasingly common feature (see Figure 5.8). If you know that you're going to need to work while you study, check what is on offer at your university. You'll generally find details on their careers service pages.

HELP WITH BUDGETING

If looking after your own finances is a new concept, you'll find lots of helpful advice on the Web. This is provided by various organizations, including banks, the NUS (see Figure 5.9) and universities themselves. All have an interest in maintaining

Do

- Ensure you sort out any entitlement to grants quickly
- Ensure you know how the student loan system works
- Budget
- Keep a record of what and where you spend
- Have a list of priority spending – differentiating between needs and wants
- Take advantage of your bank's free banking facilities
- Reply to all letters from your bank, building society or any creditors and keep a copy of all correspondence
- Acknowledge that if things go wrong financially, it can affect you emotionally and seriously distract you from your studies
- Seek advice speedily. The longer you leave a problem the harder it will be to sort it out
- Allow some money for recreation and pleasure

Don't

- Overspend at the beginning of your first term. Remember your money has to see you through the year
- Buy non-essentials when struggling to pay for essentials
- Ignore signs that spending is getting out of control
- Guess at what you are spending
- Be afraid to talk to someone and seek advice if you are having problems financially.
- Talk to family, student welfare officers, bank staff etc.
- Cut yourself off from your family and friends.
- Make rash promises to pay when you know that you can't.
- Exceed your overdraft limit without previous authorisation. Unauthorised overdraft rates are very high when compared with what is offered if you stick within agreed limits
- Get paranoid! Remember even if you are struggling, your bank or building society will see you as a good long-term investment, so approach them with confidence.

Figure 5.9 The NUS Web site has very practical budgeting suggestions

your relative financial health. However, the person who should have the greatest interest is you. Web sites listed at the end of this chapter will help you plan ahead and reduce financial worries that could detract from your enjoyment of university life. All universities have student counsellors who can advise on financial problems. You'll find details of their services on university Web sites.

STUDENT BANKING

Despite the fact that you may feel impoverished as a student, banks will be very interested in you as a customer and will court you in various ways. They recognize that today's undergraduates could be tomorrow's wealthy citizens who will then be too busy to change bank accounts. Banks like lending money – it represents a valuable source of income for them. Most banks offer students an agreed free overdraft facility, which can be anywhere between £100 and £2000 per year, with larger amounts for later years of study. The potential to run up huge debts is frightening and it's important that you are aware of charges this will incur once you have finished your studies.

Most banks offer special accounts to full-time students, with introductory promotional offers, such as free railcards (see Figure 5.10). However, you should not base your choice of bank on just these points. It's important to check:

- if interest is paid on current accounts in credit;
- special student insurance deals;
- availability of cashpoints and telephone banking;
- location of branches;
- the rates of interest charged if you go over the free overdraft limit – it can be as much as 34 per cent and can incur an extra fee of £5 a day;
- other charges once you are over the free overdraft limit – it has been known for banks to charge over £20 for each letter sent!
- what happens to your overdraft once you graduate – some banks charge current rates of interest as soon as you complete your studies; others allow you up to 12 months to repay at no interest.

You can use bank Web sites for your initial investigations, but make a personal visit to discuss the finer points. Most banks have a student adviser.

Whichever bank you choose, it is essential that you do some basic budgeting. Complete the checklist below so you can plan ahead.

STUDENT ACCOUNT

At Bank of Scotland we've created our special <u>Student Package</u> which includes an <u>interest free overdraft</u> of up to £1000 (subject to your year of study and approval from your account holding branch), our 3 in 1 **KEYCARD PLUS**, PHONELINE, our <u>free telephone banking service</u> and much, much more. <u>Check out our Student Package</u> today by calling in for a chat or telephoning your nearest Bank of Scotland Branch. Alternatively complete and return the <u>online coupon</u> and we will send you an Application Form.

STUDENT INSURANCE

With Bank of Scotland <u>Student Insurance</u>, you should still be smiling even if your life turns into a disaster movie. It's worth remembering that there are over <u>600 000 burglaries and 60 000 house fires</u> in Britain every year and with Bank of Scotland Student Insurance, you can rest easy. You receive <u>extensive cover</u> which is in force anywhere in the UK. In addition we also offer <u>"All Risks" Cover</u> and protection for your bicycle. Our <u>low cost</u> Student Insurance replaces almost everything as new <u>regardless of age</u> and last years premiums have been reduced by up to 15%. <u>Full details</u> are given in the policy avail able on request from any Bank of Scotland branch.

Figure 5.10 Banks have a range of tempting offers for students

CHECKLIST 5: EXPENDITURE AND INCOME

University:

Costs:

	£
Fee contribution	
Accommodation	
Food	
Books, equipment, other course requirements	
Electricity/gas	
Social/leisure	
Travel	
Other	
Total	

Income:

	£
Sponsorship	
University bursary	
Part-time/vacation work	
Income from sandwich year	
Student loan available	
Overdraft available	
Other	
Total	

SITES WORTH SEEING

Fees and loans

Department for Education and Employment (DfEE)
http://www.dfee.gov.uk
Up-to-date information on financial support for higher education students whose homes are in England or Wales is available here. The current advisory booklet can be downloaded. Check for details of additional financial incentives for students, such as those related to Initial Teacher Training in shortage subjects. *Bridging the Gap*, which provides information about the Disabled Students' Allowance, can be found at:

http://www.dfee.gov.uk/bridging/index.htm

NUS Student Information
http://www.nus.org.uk
Excellent information is provided on the realities of students' financial problems. Various sections of the site offer analyses, practical budgeting help and up-to-date information on latest developments.

Student Awards Agency for Scotland (SAAS)
http://www.student-support-saas.gov.uk
Information is available here for Scottish students who are studying full-time HNC, HND or first degree, PGCE and PG courses.

Student Loans Company Ltd
http://www.slc.co.uk
Everything you need to know about eligibility, amounts and repayment terms straight from the lenders.

Student Finance

Sponsorships and vacation schemes

Note: Employers and organizations referred to in this chapter are:

BBC World of Training
http://www.bbc.co.uk/jobs/maj_sch.shtml
Look here for details of major training schemes.

DERA
http://www.dera.gov.uk
Scholarships are available just for being nice about them.

Ernst & Young's summer vacation scheme
http://www.eyuk.com
Vacation opportunities for undergraduates include work shadowing, industrial placements and an office insight programme at a number of different locations.

IEE-accredited degree courses
http://www.iee.org.uk/Membship/d_accred.htm
There is a downloadable list of courses accredited by the Institute. Sponsoring employers generally require attendance on such a course. The Institute also has bursaries available for members only (see Figure 4.5).

Institute of Materials
http://www.materials.org.uk
The education pages carry careers information for materials science. There are links to a list of departments that offer a £1000 Institute of Materials bursary to a student with BBB grades at A level.

Local government student sponsorship
http://www.lgmb.gov.uk
Penultimate year sponsorship, paid vacation work and additional prizes for undergraduates from any discipline.

sites worth seeing

Shell Step Scheme

http://www.shell-step.org

Paid eight-week industrial placements are offered to degree and HND students in the summer before their final year. The scheme is aimed at students under 24 without significant work experience.

Note: Addresses for universities and professional bodies are on the NISS Web site (see Chapter 2). Employers' Web sites can be found using a search engine (see Appendix) or employer directories (see Chapter 4).

All the Armed Forces offer sponsorship and details can be found on their Web sites:

Army

http://www.army.mod.uk

Navy

http://www.royal-navy.mod.uk

RAF

http://www.raf-careers.raf.mod.uk

Charities

Charities Direct

http://www.caritasdata.co.uk

Here you will find a database of around 5000 of the UK's top charities with a large education section. The charities indicate whether or not they currently have resources available and are prepared to consider applications. There is information about and contact details for each charity (see Figure 5.11).

Fundsnet

http://www.fundsnetservices.com

This is an American organization that maintains an impressive database of links to charities and grant-making bodies worldwide. There are sections on international and education-related aid and scholarship providers, although this is predominantly for American students. These are useful for UK students wanting to study in the US. There are also excellent links to resources that can help you make effective grant applications.

Finance for higher education students				
	period	expenditure	grantmaker	grants available
British Academy	Mar-97	1 / £23.1m 100%	Yes	Yes
Hugh Pilkington Charitable Trust	Sep-97	2 / £1.46m 100%	Yes	Fully committed
Exeter University Foundation	Jul-97	3 / £0.74m 100%	Yes	Yes
Student Support Services	Mar-97	4 / £0.52m 100%		
Howell's [Thomas] Charity	Jul-97	5 / £0.45m 100%	Yes	Fully committed
Stonyhurst Charitable Fund	Sep-96	6 / £0.37m 100%	Yes	Not known
Royal Academy of Music Foundation	Mar-97	7 / £0.35m 35%	Yes	Yes
Fishmongers' Company's Charitable Trust	Dec-96	8 / £0.27m 24%	Yes	Yes
Martin's [John] Charity	Mar-97	8 / £0.27m 46%	Yes	Yes
Karten [Ian] Charitable Trust	Sep-97	10 / £0.26m 28%	Yes	Yes
Mercers' Company Educational Trust Fund	Jul-97	11 / £0.26m 100%	Yes	Not known
Datchelor [Mary] Trust	Dec-96	12 / £0.14m 100%	Yes	Yes
Sino-British Fellowship Trust	Dec-95	13 / £0.13m 100%	Yes	Not known
Perry [Sidney] Foundation	Dec-96	14 / £0.13m 100%	Yes	Yes
Royal Pinner School Foundation	Mar-97	15 / £0.09m 31%	Yes	Yes

Figure 5.11 Charities Direct can be searched by name or sector

Student banking

National Association for Managers of Student Services in Colleges (NAMSS)

http://www.namss.org.uk/banks.htm

The student finance section of this site has an excellent table of comparative costs for student bank accounts. It provides an overview and links to all the banks (see Figure 5.12).

sites worth seeing

Student bank accounts,
young people's bank accounts
& graduate bank accounts & overdrafts

This page is updated monthly from information provided by "**Moneyfacts**", but please note that rates may change at short notice.

PLEASE NOTE: The Bank of England reduced interest rates on 4th February & it is possible that some banks may change their rates before our next update at the beginning of March.

These charts should not be seen as advice and you should check directly with the banks you are interested in. However, we recommend that you look at issues such as interest on your money if you are in credit, overdraft rates & charges for services as well as looking at incentives.

All rates are variable and shown gross. Overdraft rates and fees only apply on overdrawn balances above the interest-free limit.

- **Student Bank Accounts**
- **Graduate Bank Accounts**
- **Finance for international students**

- Student loans scheme
- Graduate loans
- Student Finance Index

- Other loans for education
- **Young People's Accounts**
- NAMSS Site Index

Figure 5.12 You can get an up-to-date overview of student banking here

Study Outside the UK

There is increased interest in studying abroad, either as part of a UK degree course or in its own right. The Internet takes the hard work and delay out of the necessary research and communication.

- Overseas study as part of a UK degree course
- Independently arranged overseas study
- Special concerns
- Sites worth seeing

In a global employment market, the chance to spend some time abroad is valuable. Experience and insight gained from living and studying in another country can significantly enhance your future career prospects. The fact that you have participated in and successfully completed such a scheme sends a clear signal to employers that you are motivated, self-reliant, able to take the initiative and have an awareness of other cultures – all skills that they are looking for.

Internet-based resources can help you quickly identify courses that offer these opportunities. Its easy to make a 'virtual' visit to any university in the world, obtain course and admissions information and have a look around the locality at the same time. Universities market themselves as efficiently as any tourist attraction. All have pages designed to attract international students, giving detailed information on the formalities and incorporating links to help you find out about living and studying in their country.

OVERSEAS STUDY AS PART OF A UK DEGREE COURSE

The simplest way to arrange overseas study is to choose a degree course that incorporates a year abroad. The most common links are between universities in the European Union. Many institutions also have relationships with American and Commonwealth universities, which have the advantage of being English-speaking!

Degrees where study abroad is an integral part of the course

Hospitality management students at Thames Valley can spend time in the Caribbean; theology and religious studies students from Bristol at a Tibetan monastery in India; and physics students at Salford a year in America (see Figure 3.9). It's an area that's changing all the time as new partnerships are made. Web-based prospectuses and departmental pages allow you to find who is offering what and where. If the course that interests you does not have information about international links, e-mail the course tutor to check the position.

Particularly valuable are international courses that enable you to gain dual qualifications – one from your home country and one from the partner country. It's important to check this at an early stage. Some only give a certificate of completion. More marketable, though, is a nationally recognized qualification, such as the French Maitrise or Italian Laurea (see Figure 6.1).

Erasmus

The philosopher Erasmus of Rotterdam chose to live and work in several parts of Europe, believing it would give him valuable experience and insights. That was in the fifteenth

---

Special Features

This degree is a joint venture with institutions of higher education in France, Germany, Italy and Spain. Our current partner institutions are:

France
- Universite de Savoie
- Universite Blaise-Pascal
- Universite de Bourgogne
- Sup de Co Montpellier

Germany
- Fachhochschule Bochum

Italy
- Universita Degli Studi Della Calabria

Spain
- Universidad de Murcia

Upon successfully completing this course of study, students will be awarded nationally recognised qualifications. The qualification from our partners is at least the equivalent of a British Bachelor's degree. Consequently, students who successful finish the course of study will receive the BA (Hons) Business in Europe and a Maitrise, or equivalent (French route), or a Diplom-Betriebswirt (German route), or a Laurea, or equivalent (Italian route) or a Licenciatura (Spanish route).

Figure 6.1 Graduates from the international business course at Manchester Metropolitan are in a strong position to compete for posts in multinational companies

century. Today, the scheme named after him gives European undergraduates the same opportunities. Universities develop partnerships within the EU and provide a framework for students to study at another European university.

Whatever the subject of your degree, you have the opportunity to spend time abroad as a result of the Erasmus scheme, which is available in all UK universities. Around 60,000 students participate in the scheme every year, 11,000 from the UK.

Language requirements

Tuition is in the language of the host country. UK universities provide related language courses, both for those who have previous knowledge and complete beginners. Partner universities often provide further language tuition. Developing subject-related fluency in another language gives you an extremely marketable skill for the future.

Study abroad is for between three months and a full academic year. Potentially, this can involve exchanges to any of the 15 member states of the EU, the three EEA countries of Iceland, Liechtenstein and Norway and six associated countries of Hungary, Romania, the Czech Republic, the Slovak Republic, Poland and Cyprus. Future participation is being negotiated with Bulgaria, Estonia, Latvia, Lithuania and Slovenia.

In practice, you will have a more limited choice of destinations. If a European exchange is important to you, check the links courses have at an early stage.

Grants

The home university gives a grant designed to help offset the 'mobility costs', such as travel, language preparation and differences in the cost of living. Each university administers its own system and the amount depends on your destination, the type of course you are studying and how much money the university has in proportion to the number of students who want to go. If language study is not an essential part of your course, then you get more money! For example, a single Honours chemistry degree student will receive about 2000 ECU for a full academic year. However, a chemistry and German combined degree student, for whom the study of German is a necessary part of the course, would only receive approximately 600 ECU.

Any student who spends a full academic year on an Erasmus scheme will not have to pay the UK tuition fee for that period. Otherwise, they will have to pay the full amount they are assessed for to their home university. Host universities do not charge their guest students a fee.

To check Erasmus arrangements, use the university's Web site. Most have an Erasmus or international affairs officer who will be able to help you with queries not answered on the site.

Erasmus Student Network (ESN)

In addition to formal EU and university information services, there is the active Student Network. This was founded in Copenhagen in 1990 and has branches in most countries. These provide support for incoming students by means of a 'mentor system'. The aim is to:

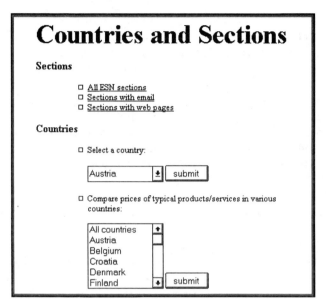

Figure 6.2 ESN provides valuable information and a discussion forum

- improve the social integration of foreign students at the host institution;
- provide information about exchange programmes;
- contribute to the evaluation of the European exchange programmes based on the experiences of former exchange students.

A visit to its Web site is a must for students interested in taking part in any European exchange programme. By using the chat and mailing list facilities you can get answers to your questions from students who've been there and done that. They also provide practical information on issues such as the comparative costs of living (see Figure 6.2).

Other international links

Universities develop many different partnerships across the world. These are often subject-related, such as the University of Central Lancashire's links with universities in China, Japan and Hong Kong for its Asia Pacific studies degree. Partnerships can involve the whole institution. For example, Imperial College is a member of Cluster, a grouping of 11 European technical institutions that are centres of excellence. Where a university or one of its departments has such established contacts, it facilitates exchange at undergraduate and postgraduate level. When selecting courses, it can be useful to investigate the international links that exist and consider the opportunities these may offer you in the future.

INDEPENDENTLY ARRANGED OVERSEAS STUDY

In theory, you can decide to study for the whole of your degree in any part of the world. In practice, it's easier and cheaper to study in your home country and incorporate a year abroad. If, however, your circumstances or aspirations are such that study outside the UK is more appropriate to you, then the Internet is an unsurpassable resource for researching and arranging it, as every university has a Web site.

Finding basic information

UNESCO maintains a publicly accessible database of world universities (see Figure 6.3). It gives an overview of education systems in every country in the world and can be used to gather basic facts and obtain contact details for further investigation. The sections on higher education cover cost of living, tuition and financial arrangements for foreign students.

Braintrack (see Figure 1.8) provides a quick search and link facility for universities worldwide. The range and quality of material from each will vary, but there is always enough to give you an insight. Use Checklist 3 in Chapter 3 to help you identify what you need to investigate.

Finance is obviously going to be an important consideration and universities always have pages for international students that give information on what help is available, although funds are limited. Many international university Web sites have an English version, but it would be a good test of your language skills to access the site in the home language. If you can't cope with that, you wont be able to cope with the study either. Most universities will ask you to undertake a language proficiency test before applying.

Special entry regulations for foreign students

Foreign students intending to study in New Zeland should contact the nearest New Zealand embassy or high commission to obtain information on visa regulations. There is a charge for student visa based on NZ$ 190,00. Police clearances are also required.

Application to national/central body:
Individual applicants must be sent to the universities of the student's choice.

Earliest application closing date for foreign students admissions
For first university level studies: 1 September

Reference to further information materials on foreign students admissions
Title: Tertiary education in New Zeland
Publisher: New Zealand Education International Ltd

Is there a national social security system health insurance for home students?
Up to 2 years, foreign students must pay 100% of health care costs. For 3 or more years, foreign students are treated as New Zealanders, the government pays 75–80% of health-care costs.

Special travel concessions for students:

By road:	Yes
By rail:	Yes
By air:	Yes
Is it available for foreign students?	Yes

Student expenses and financial aid
Average living costs for current academic year: New Zealand Dollar 16,000

Tuition and fees for foreign students

Minimum: New Zealand Dollar	5,000
Maximum: New Zealand Dollar	40,000

Financial aid

Grants for foreign students	Yes
Grants for home students	Yes
Loans for foreign students	No
Loans for home students	Yes

Figure 6.3   UNESCO's World Academic Database gives an overview of every higher education system

Language requirements

You have to be fluent in the subject you will be studying. Even being a native speaker does not guarantee that you will have the vocabulary to understand a thermodynamics lecture. Academic discussion groups abound on the Internet, as do learned societies with their numerous publications (see Chapter 2). You can privately test your subject-related language skills by reading these in the language of the country you hope to study in. If this is a bit daunting, there is a huge choice of study options available in the English-speaking world.

Comparability of qualifications

Evaluating the quality of a course is always a problem. Some countries have carried out comparative studies and these can be accessed via newspapers such as *Der Spiegel* in Germany or *US News* in America (see Figure 6.7). Governments' education department Web sites may also carry such information. Locate these using country-specific search engines with the search string 'university rankings' (see Appendix).

As well as looking at course content, costs and quality, you need to investigate:

- the acceptability of your qualifications to overseas universities;
- the international acceptability of qualifications you hope to gain.

In the UK and other EU member states, information on this is provided by National Academic Recognition Centres (NARIC). Contact details can be found on the Europa Web site (the address is given in the Sites worth seeing section at the end of this chapter).

Another resource for investigating the comparability of professional qualifications across Europe is the Citizens EU Web site (see Figures 6.4 and 8.3). Most professional bodies have international links and can advise on qualifications in their own field. An international database of learned societies, maintained by the University of Waterloo in Canada, provides a comprehensive list of organizations worldwide that would be able to advise on their specialism (see Figure 2.9).

European rights of access

All citizens of EU states have the right to study at the higher education institutions of any other member state. They are eligible for the same fee support as nationals, but not any maintenance support. As a UK citizen, you can apply to study for a university course in any member state. In reality, there are many barriers to doing this. Assuming fluency in the language, problems can include:

- finance;
- different academic structures;
- different attitudes to student life;
- loneliness and isolation.

As a citizen of the European Union (EU) you have many rights that you may not be aware of. Did you know, for example, that you can go to any other EU country to study, work or retire, while enjoying the same rights as nationals of that country?

The EU is publishing this series of guides explaining your rights so that you can make the most of the opportunities available to you. The guides also point out the conditions attached to your rights. The scope and diversity of these rights is so great that a brief description of them cannot hope to take in every individual situation. If you require any additional information, please do not hesitate to get in touch with one of the contact points listed under point IV. Useful adresses.

Each factsheet covers one country and describes what you have to do there to use your rights.

For example, the factsheet on the Right of residence explains, in your own language, how to obtain a residence permit in the country you study in. To obtain any factsheets, dial the freephone number given on this website. You will be answered in English.

Figure 6.4 The Citizens EU site makes it easy to obtain facts about study in the EU

Finance

If you study for the whole of your degree at a European university, you will pay the same fees as a national of that country. In some cases, such as in the Republic of Ireland, there is no fee. If the student contribution to fees is means-tested, as in the UK, you will have to apply for support to the education authority in the area where you hope to study. You will not be eligible for a maintenance grant or loan scheme from that country, nor would you get a student loan from the UK scheme. Any institution you are applying to will be able to give you more detailed advice on the procedures and contacts.

The one exception to this is the British Institute in Paris (http://www.bip.lon.ac.uk), which is part of the University of London. It is regarded as part of the UK system, so normal UK funding regulations apply.

Academic structures

European universities generally have larger teaching groups and a greater dependence on printed course material than UK ones. British students may find the system more impersonal, with less contact between tutor and student than is the norm in the UK. European countries also make more use of oral examinations – even public oral examinations – for assessment. In Italy, for example, the majority of the exams are oral. Students surviving this experience can easily prove they have the sophisticated communication skills employers are looking for.

The time it takes to complete your study is also a consideration. Degrees in the UK are among the shortest in the world. In many other countries, it is common to graduate in your mid to late twenties. Longer periods of study can mean longer periods of financial hardship.

Student life

Student support services, such as accommodation, careers and welfare services, which are well developed in the UK, may be less so in other countries. For example, it is more common for students to live in the family home while they study in many European countries than is the case in the UK. UK universities are reputed to offer the best social life, but then they don't have easy access to world-class ski resorts or warm weather. As with all aspects of higher education choice, you have to decide what's important to you, what's realistic, and then investigate all the options.

Isolation

This can be a problem for all students, whether they study at home or abroad. Investigate the support services available for foreign students and find out how many there are. International offices should be able to put you in touch with current students from your country to enable you to find out what it's really like.

Formalities for study outside the EU

Many students are drawn to other English-speaking countries, such as the USA, Canada and Australia, but UK citizens do not have an automatic right of residence in countries outside the EU. Where overseas study is with a scholarship, residence permits are usually granted automatically. If you are financing yourself, however, you will have to apply for a permit and prove that you have sufficient funds. In some cases, student visas can only be obtained after careful scrutiny of your means and may prevent you from working legally. You will also have to prove that you have adequate health insurance cover in countries that do not have reciprocal health agreements with the UK.

Scholarships for UK students to study abroad exist for some countries and some courses. If you have particular universities in mind, their international student advisers will give you help and guidance. You can, in addition, investigate for yourself using:

● on-line student funding databases (see Chapter 5);

Studying in the United States: You need a student visa to attend an American university or other academic institution, including secondary and vocational schools. You must first be accepted by the school which must issue you a form I–20 'Certificate of Eligibility' before you can apply for the visa. US law prohibits issuance of F–1 visas for public elementary school studies or publicly funded adult education programs, and limits students attending public secondary schools to no more than 12 months of public high school in F–1 visa status.

Detailed information on some visa categories:

U.S. Visa Requirements for Academics, Researchers & Exchange Students

B–1/B–2 Visas for Temporary Visitors

Temporary Work Visa (H & L)

Visa Requirements for Members of the Media (I visas)

Exchange Visitor Visa (J–1)

O Visas for Aliens with Exceptional Abilities; P visas for Athletes, Artists and Entertainers

Figure 6.5 Embassy Web sites can help you investigate the formalities

- the international students section of your intended university's Web site;
- embassy Web sites – these are also useful for checking visa formalities (see Figure 6.5);
- the British Council and Central Bureau for Educational Visits and Exchanges Web sites (the address is given in the Sites worth seeing section at the end of this chapter).

Related schemes

These are organized by bodies other than universities and give students a chance to combine study, work and travel. Many professional and vocational areas have international student organizations that facilitate exchange and networking around the world. A selection of these are listed at the end of this chapter.

SPECIAL CONCERNS

Having a disability or special need should not be a barrier to making use of international opportunities. You can use the

Web to explore your options, make arrangements and sort out potential problems at a distance. The Europa Web site (see Figures 3.12 and 6.6) provides excellent help for disabled students. Its checklist can be downloaded and used as a questionnaire to send to overseas universities. You can look at it in your own language, download a version in the language of your host country and send that as an e-mail.

Europa's *European Guide for Students with Disabilities* gives information on specialized provision for disabled students and contact details for disability coordinators in most universities in Europe.

Information for disabled students planning to study abroad

In the framework of the HELIOS II programme for the integation of disabled persons the European Commission (DGV) has supported the production of a two-volume study 'Studying Abroad', designed to facilitate the mobility of disabled students in higher education.

Volume 1: **Checklist of needs for students with disabilities** contains structured information to help students with disabilities gain a clearer idea of the sort of facilities available at their planned host university to facilitate physical and pedagogical access to study. The checklist will also help higher education institutions make the necessary arrangements for study visits by disabled students. It is available in all 11 official Community languages. The checklist can be downloaded from this site by following the link.

Volume 2: **European guide for students with disabilities** is a directory containing details of facilities and guidance services available in some 235 universities in Europe. It is available in English, with an English/French glossary. The European guide can be downloaded from this site by following the **link**.

Figure 6.6   These two comprehensive guides are simply formatted and quick to download

If you're planning on going further afield, you will find similar information and provision for disabled students at most universities in the world. Their Web sites are good starting points, but if you can't find the information, e-mail their international department.

CHECKLIST 6: UK DEGREES OVERSEAS OPPORTUNITIES CHECKLIST
Web resources to use
University:
Course:
Erasmus: *University/departmental Web site*
Links to:
Duration:
Language tuition:
Additional costs:
Likely mobility grant:
What other students say: *Erasmus Student Network*
Other international links: *University/departmental Web site*
Dual qualifications available:
Language skills required:
Cost/financial help available:
The partner institution: *University/departmental Web site*
Highlights:
Number of overseas students:
Quality assessment:
Critical comparison and university rankings sites
Accommodation details:
Possible drawbacks:

You need to evaluate overseas degrees methodically, too.

Identify the overseas opportunities for your chosen course by filling in the above checklist.

CHECKLIST 7: OVERSEAS DEGREES

Web resources to use

University:
Braintrack

Course:
National course databases (such as, Study Link Australia, CIES France)

Entry requirements:
Course databases/university Web site

Language requirements:
University Web site

Application procedures:
UNESCO World Academic Database
University Web site

Course structure:
University Web site
(See also Checklist 3, page 73)

Assessment methods:
University Web site
(See also Checklist 4, page 89)

Comparability of degree-level qualification:
Citizens EU
Professional bodies
NARIC

The formalities:

Immigration requirements:
Immigration department
University Web site
Embassy Web site

Cost of study: *University Web site*
Cost of living: *University Web site* *(See also Checklist 5, page 113)*
Financial help available: *Fundsnet* *Education department* *University Web site*
The university:
Highlights:
Number of overseas students: *University Web site*
Quality assessment: *Critical comparison and university rankings sites*
Student services: *University Web site* *Students union*
Accommodation details: *University Web site*
Possible drawbacks:
Special concerns: *Europa* *University Web site*
Why study overseas?

———— SITES WORTH SEEING ————

Europe

Association des Etats Généraux des Etudiants de l'Europe

http://www.aegee.org
This is the association of European student unions.

Central Applications Office (CAO) for the Republic of Ireland

http://indigo.ie/~cao
The office processes applications for degree courses in the Irish Republic. The closing date is in February. Late applications are possible until May, but incur an increased fee. There are links to the Web sites of all the participating institutions.

Citizens EU

http://citizens.eu.int
This is a well-organized site that allows you to enter your country of origin and the country you want to investigate. There is information on work and education opportunities in each member state. There is also detailed information on comparability of professional qualifications and the facility to order or download related booklets (see Figures 6.4 and 8.3).

DfEE – The European Choice 1998–99

http://www.dfee.gov.uk/dfee/echoice/index.htm
Information is available on all aspects of study in Europe for UK students.

Erasmus Student Network (ESN)

http://www.esn.org
Visit this site for all the inside information on Erasmus from students who've done it (see Figure 6.2).

Europa Database

http://europa.eu.int/index-en.htm
This is a huge resource. It is regularly updated, so specific URLs may change. The above takes you to an English language index. To find all the information you need on Erasmus and NARIC, use the search engine from the index page.

Information for disabled students on studying abroad can be found at:

`http://europa.eu.int/en/comm/dg22/socrates/`
`specnds.html`

For a checklist of the needs of students with disabilities see:

`http://europa.eu.int/en/comm/dg22/socrates/`
`chklst.html`

Also available is a European guide for students with disabilities (see Figures 3.12 and 6.6).

Centre International des Etudiants et Stagiaires (CIES)

`http://www.cies.fr`
Information on French education and training opportunities for foreign students and researchers can be found here. The course database and background information on study and life in France is available in both French and English.

German Academic Exchange Service (DAAD)

`http://www.daad.de`
This site provides comprehensive information on all aspects of higher education study for foreign nationals in Germany. Included are details of scholarships, funding and schemes for summer language tuition.

The rest of the world

American Embassy London Visa Services

`http://www.usembassy.org.uk/ukvisas.html`
Information on student visas can be found here (see Figure 6.5).

Association of Universities and Colleges of Canada

`http://www.aucc.ca`
See this site for links, resources and information about Canadian higher education.

Braintrack

http://www.braintrack.com

Based in Switzerland, this site offers over 4500 links to higher education institutions in 148 countries (see Figure 1.8).

Bureau of Educational and Cultural Affairs – US Information Agency

http://e.usia.gov/education

This site provides prospective students with information and guidance on US higher education via a network of educational advising centres.

Critical comparisons of American colleges and universities

http://www.memex-press.com/cc/index.html

This site includes all the usual data on academic performance and additional information on issues such as campus crime.

US News college rankings

http://www.usnews.com/usnews/edu/college/corank.htm

These are superficially similar to *The Times'* rankings, but, as well as comparing academic matters, you can rank colleges by best marching bands, football team or snowfall (see Figure 6.7).

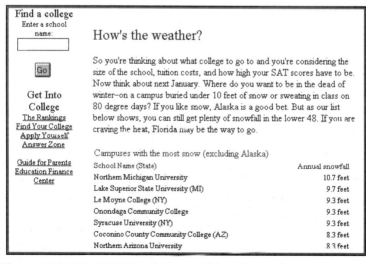

Figure 6.7   The *US News* league tables think of everything!

sites worth seeing

Embassy Page
http://www.embpage.org
This is a searchable site with links to most embassies and consulates in all parts of the world.

Fulbright Commission
http://www.fulbright.co.uk
Everything you need to know about study in the USA. This is a well-organized site that shows you all the possibilities and highlights and gives solutions to some of the problems.

Peterson's Education Center
http://www.petersons.com/ac
A database of all educational institutions in the US with lots of links to related information and sites.

Study Link Australia
http://www.studylink.com.au
A comprehensive guide to Australian higher education. The course database covers 260 institutions and over 10,000 courses. There are links to advice from student counsellors via an on-line enquiry form.

The World Academic Database
http://www.unesco.org/iau/wad.html
There is information on every educational system in the world here (see Figure 6.3).

Related schemes

AIESEC
http://www.aiesec.org
The site offers international exchange programmes to students as part of their mission to develop individuals to take a leading role in the global marketplace. Opportunities for UK students include its International Traineeship Exchange, Work Abroad and Management Training schemes. These are aimed at business studies students.

Central Bureau for Educational Visits and Exchanges

http://www.britcoun.org/cbeve

Details of exchange and work placement schemes for university students can be found on the site's programmes for further and higher education pages. These include a range of paid English teaching opportunities and bursaries for self-devised projects.

Council in Europe

http://www.ciee.org/europe

The Council offers work experience, short-term jobs and exchange programmes in a wide range of countries for students and recent graduates. Each year, over 20,000 students, the majority Europeans, participate in these programmes, including the Japan Exchange and Teaching programme (JET) and the US Internship scheme.

International Association for the Exchange of Students for Technical Experience (IAESTE)

http://www.iaeste.org

The Association arranges course-related work placements for undergraduates in science, engineering and technology. The majority of these are summer placements. The employers pay a salary, but students pay their own travel costs.

Applications and the Internet

The process of applying for higher education in the United Kingdom is centralized and regulated. You can use the Internet to obtain detailed information on all the procedures and to help you produce an effective application.

- The mechanics of applying
- Special concerns
- The art of applying
- Clearing
- Sites worth seeing

THE MECHANICS OF APPLYING

For most higher education courses in the UK, applications are made using a centralized system. The systems are:

- UCAS – for degree, HND and Dip HE courses in the UK;
- NMAS – nursing diplomas in England;
- CATCH – nursing diplomas in Scotland;
- SWAS – diploma-level courses in social work in the UK.

Applications for diploma-level nursing courses in Wales are made directly to individual institutions. The Nursing Board for Wales provides information on all of these courses.

UCAS

Every last detail of the UCAS application system is thoroughly explained on its web site (see Figure 7.1). There are special sections for international and mature students as well as comprehensive information for all UK applicants.

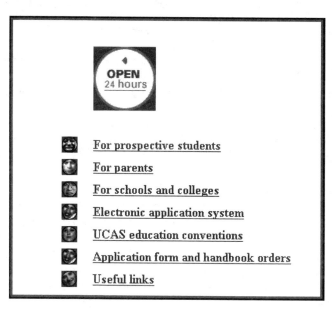

Figure 7.1 The UCAS Web site has all the information you need to help you with the formalities of applying

The basics are that:

- you can apply for up to six courses;
- all applications are treated equally – you do not express a preference;
- the application period is from September to 15 December of the year before you hope to start your course;
- late applications are accepted until 30 June – after that, all applications go through clearing;
- a clearing system that matches vacancies with applicants operates from mid July until the end of September.

Application for up to six courses is done on one form. If you are a student at a UK school or college, you have to use forms from that institution. Mature students can obtain an application pack from careers offices or the UCAS web site. Overseas students can get their application pack from their local British Council office or the UCAS web site.

All the necessary materials are distributed free of charge to UK and EU applicants, but other overseas students are charged for the application pack. Also:

- all students are charged an application fee – currently £5 for one course and £14 for more than one;
- you can only submit one form during the application cycle;
- once you have submitted your form, it's very difficult to make changes to your choices unless there are exceptional circumstances.

Offers

UCAS sends a copy of your form to the universities you have chosen and each makes its own decision about your application. It is increasingly uncommon for universities to interview 'standard' applicants – decisions are often made on the content of the application form. These are sent to UCAS and UCAS then notify you. If you submit your form by 15 December, you will have all your decisions by the end of April. If you are a late applicant (16 December to 30 June), you will have final decisions at the end of July. Possible outcomes are:

- **Unconditional offer** The university will offer you a place without you having to do anything else. If you have an unconditional offer and accept it, you may not accept other offers.
- **Conditional offer** If you have exams to take or studies to complete, you are likely to be made a conditional offer. This will specify the conditions you will need to meet to be offered a place. They usually, but not always, consist of exam grades. If you have conditional offers, you may accept two – one you confirm as a firm acceptance, the other as insurance.

- **Change of course, change of year, change of point of entry** Universities can offer an alternative course, entry in the following year or changed point of entry. They would normally discuss this with you first.
- **Rejection** This means they are not going to offer you a place. That decision is final, and neither the university nor UCAS are required to give reasons for it.

Once you have replied to your offers, you cannot easily change your mind. For degrees, you should therefore only accept offers for courses you really want to study.

- If you accept a conditional offer for a degree firmly or as insurance and it is later confirmed, you will not be able to decline it in order to enter clearing.
- If your firmly accepted conditional offer is confirmed, your insurance offer is automatically cancelled.

This is not the case for HND offers – even if you hold an offer, you can enter clearing to try get a place on a degree course.

Confirmation

Exam results are automatically sent to UCAS by the examination boards, and if you have achieved the grades your place will be confirmed by UCAS. If you have met the conditions of your offer, the university is obliged to give you a place on that course, even if it is oversubscribed (see NHS bursaries, Chapter 5). If you don't get the grades asked for, you may still be offered a place by one of your choices. It's worth contacting the institution to see how it reacts to your results. Details of clearing and how to contact universities during this period are explained later in this chapter.

Art and design applications

There are two application routes – A and B – for art and design courses. In total, you can apply for six courses, which can be all via route A or a combination of A and B, but with a maximum of four choices via route B. All applicants for art and design courses need a portfolio of work. Route A applications are processed in the same way as other UCAS applications. The main differences for route B are that:

- applications are made between 1 January and 24 March of the year you intend to start studying;
- you can choose a maximum of four courses;
- you complete an interview preference form in addition to your UCAS form – this shows the order in which you wish to be interviewed and UCAS sends your form to institutions in the order you choose.

If you are applying via route A and B and you complete your form before 1 January, you only enter your route A choices, ticking the appropriate box to show that you will subsequently apply for route B courses. You then get another form from UCAS later for this. When you complete the second form, you have the opportunity to update your personal statement and reference.

Electronic application system

UCAS operates an electronic application system. It is not currently available to individuals, but must be used through a school, college, careers centre or British Council office (for overseas applicants). There are plans to make it available via the Internet in the future. This system allows you to complete your application on a computer and send it to UCAS via the Internet or disk. If you have access to this option, its advantages over paper are that:

- the form can be processed more quickly by UCAS;
- it removes the potential distraction of hard-to-read handwriting;
- it's better designed for showing GNVQ and BTEC units;
- the program automatically checks for common errors;
- you can paste your personal statement into the form from a word processor.

Oxford and Cambridge

There are many myths and misconceptions surrounding these two institutions, and some students are either put off or attracted to them on the basis of these. Although they have demanding entry requirements, both universities encourage

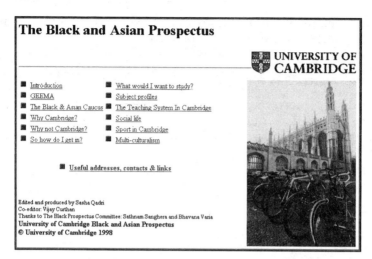

The Black and Asian Prospectus

UNIVERSITY OF CAMBRIDGE

- Introduction
- GEEMA
- The Black & Asian Caucus
- Why Cambridge?
- Why not Cambridge?
- So how do I get in?

- What would I want to study?
- Subject profiles
- The Teaching System In Cambridge
- Social life
- Sport in Cambridge
- Multi-culturalism

- Useful addresses, contacts & links

Edited and produced by Sasha Qadri
Co-editor: Vijay Curthan
Thanks to The Black Prospectus Committee: Sathnam Sanghera and Bhavana Varia
University of Cambridge Black and Asian Prospectus
© University of Cambridge 1998

Figure 7.2   Look at alternative prospectuses produced by students as well as the institutional ones

applications from all backgrounds. What they have to offer does not suit everyone. If you are interested in finding out more, there's no better place to start than their Web sites (see Figure 7.2). They allow you to make initial judgements on virtual realities! Both universities have excellent sites for the whole institution and for individual colleges.

Oxford and Cambridge interview all candidates and, as they have more well-qualified applicants than places, decisions are made on personal attributes as well as academic excellence. They are looking for interested and interesting individuals who are able both to form and defend their own opinions and respond well to intellectual challenge.

If you are applying to Oxford or Cambridge, you need to:

- submit a completed Oxford application card to the Oxford Colleges Admissions Office by 15 October;
- submit a completed preliminary application form to the Admissions Tutor of the Cambridge college listed as first choice or, in the case of an open application, to the Cambridge Intercollegiate Applications Office, by 15 October;
- submit your UCAS form by 15 October.

You cannot apply to both Oxford and Cambridge, unless you are applying for an organ scholarship.

Nurses and Midwives Admissions Service (NMAS)

NMAS processes applications for full-length, diploma-level pre-registration nursing and midwifery programmes in England (see Figure 7.3). It does not deal with nursing degrees – these are processed by UCAS.

NMAS Home			
	Course directory	Start dates	Course code
	All courses have vacancies		
	Univ Of Central Lancashire		
Click onto an institution title for further information	Adult Nursing	March, September	3000
	Mental Health Nursing	March, September	3100
	Children's Nursing	September	3300
	University College Chester		
	Midwifery	February, September	1800
	Adult Nursing	March, September	3000
	Mental Health Nursing	March, September	3100
	Learning Disability Nursing	September	3200
	Children's Nursing	March, September	3300
	City University		
	Adult Nursing	March, September	3000
	Mental Health Nursing	March, September	3100
	Children's Nursing	March, September	3300

Figure 7.3 NMAS provides access to all the information you need. Application packs can be ordered on-line

In addition to information on application procedures, there are links to all institutions offering nursing diploma courses in England. As each institution sets its own entry requirements, which may exceed the minimum, you need to check each one before selecting it as one of your four choices. The site also carries details of current course vacancies.

The main features are that:

● the earliest age for application is 16 – you cannot start nurse training until you are 17½;

- you need to have the statutory qualifications before applying – no conditional offers are made;
- you can only accept one offer;
- the minimum educational requirements are five GCSEs – grades A–C, or equivalent; midwifery applicants must include English language or literature plus a science or mathematics;
- you can apply for up to four courses – you don't indicate a preference as all choices are treated equally;
- the application period is between September and 15 December for the following year – late applications are accepted until 30 June;
- most institutions have spring and autumn intakes, so it may be possible to be offered a place in the spring following your application if there are free places, but you may have to wait until the following year – for example, a student submitting an application in September 2000 may be offered a place in spring 2001, autumn 2001, spring 2002 or autumn 2002;
- NMAS operates a clearing system for unfilled vacancies from July to September, and applicants can also contact institutions directly at that point;
- there is a standard application fee (currently £10), but those who only apply for one course pay a reduced fee (£5).

CATCH

This organization provides a similar service to NMAS for those who wish to do their nurse training in Scotland (see Figure 7.4). The main differences arc that:

- students can begin nurse training at the age of 17;
- the four chosen courses are listed in order of preference and submitted to institutions accordingly;
- there is no application fee;
- there is no set application period, but most institutions will not consider applicants more than 12 months before the start date of the course.

Figure 7.4 Nursing applications for Scotland are made via CATCH

Social Work Application System (SWAS)

SWAS processes applications for non-graduate and postgraduate college-based social work programmes. These are generally for mature students with related work experience. The SWAS application pack can be ordered from the UCAS web site. The application period is September to 15 December for courses starting the following year. General information on social work training can be found on the Central Council for Education and Training in Social Work's (CCETSW) Web site (see Chapter 2).

SPECIAL CONCERNS

Some students worry about disclosing a disability when applying for a higher education course. Details are asked for by institutions to prepare for meeting your special requirements. This could mean arranging building adaptations, volunteer helpers or equipment for you. The information you provide is treated confidentially by the university and does not affect judgements concerning your academic suitability. It may also explain some other aspects of your application, such as having taken longer over courses. The sooner an institution is aware of your needs, the sooner it can investigate ways of meeting them.

If you feel that you encounter discrimination in relation to your disability, then you're better off avoiding that institution all together. The central admissions agencies will allow you extra choices if you receive a rejection based on your disability.

Your application should aim to show that your disability does not impair your intellectual abilities. Explain how your disability affects you and the strategies you have developed to cope with that. It's good to show that you have thought about the potential problems and ways they can be overcome with support. Most universities interview all disabled applicants and this is an excellent opportunity for you to find out if the course and place will be suitable.

THE ART OF APPLYING

It's essential that your application is well thought out, well presented and does justice to your abilities and aspirations. Make sure you read the accompanying notes carefully and always work on a photocopy first. If you are completing your form by hand, make sure it is neat and legible. Forms are copied and reduced in size before being forwarded to institutions. All application forms use both sides of a page, so choose a pen that will not leak through the paper!

Timing

Where there is a closing date, applications are supposed to be treated equally until that time. This does not always happen in practice. Students who apply in September or October will often start to receive offers in November. Admissions tutors do not want to be swamped at the end of December and so they start to consider applications as soon as they receive them. If you feel ready to make an effective application, early submission of your form gives you an advantage. The admissions services and universities process forms more quickly when they have fewer to deal with. As the application cycle progresses, therefore, the number of places available decreases.

Research

You should only submit your application once you have thoroughly researched your choices and can make a strong case for your suitability. Your application needs to be realistic in terms of the entry requirements and your predicted grades. It also needs to show that you are aware of what the courses involve and lead to. If you are not able to communicate this effectively, look at Chapters 2 and 3 again.

As well as research based on reading, if you are applying for courses with a strong vocational element, admissions tutors want to see that you have gained first-hand experience through placements and visits to the relevant profession.

You can use Web-based information to research the interests and achievements of those who will be considering your application and, if you are successful, teaching you. It's possible to find out who teaches what in a university department and read a brief biography, full CV or all their published works (see Figure 3.11). Lecturers want students they can relate to and enjoy teaching. If you share interests, then all the better.

Realism

An admissions tutor's main concern is that students offered a place should be able to cope with the study and complete it successfully. After all, the degree grades achieved by students affect their ranking in future years! You need to be fair to yourself, too, and only apply for courses you can cope with. Your reference will include your academic potential and the grades you are expected to get. These should be in line with the entry requirements of the courses. Check with those who know your academic abilities that your choices are realistic. It's normal for students to choose at least one course that is likely to ask for slightly lower entry requirements than they hope to get. This is the one you would keep as your insurance offer. However, it shouldn't be too much lower. If a university thinks you'd only go to them as a last resort, they may not offer you a place.

Compatibility of courses selected

Every course for which you apply receives a copy of your application form and can therefore see every other course for which you have applied. If you apply for a range of subject areas, you are advertising your uncertainty about preferences for further study and are unlikely to be offered a place. This does not mean you have to apply for only one subject, but the courses you apply for should be related. You could, for example, apply for courses that cover a range of biological sciences or mix applications for sport science courses with a sport teaching qualification. Your selection should show a clear preference for a particular subject area or career aim that is then explained in your personal statement.

Personal statement

All application forms have a section for you to explain why you should be offered a place on your chosen course. Many students find this the most difficult and daunting part of the form. There is excellent general information on what should be included in a personal statement on the UCAS web site and many university departments give additional guidance on their Web pages for prospective applicants (see Figure 7.5).

As well as following those guidelines, aim to leave the reader with the following:

- A glimpse of your personality. Many students feel they have to use very formal language. That can come across as forced and stilted or a repetition of phrases used by

focus your statement
- *concentrate on your intellectual and cultural interests:* don't spend more than (say) the last 20% of the statement on those things which make you a 'rounded' person (e.g. service to school or community, sporting activities, charity work). Mature applicants in particular should note this difference from the more general personal statements expected for access and preparatory courses.
- *if you're applying for Combined Honours, express and explain your interest in both courses:* admissions tutors are suspicious – sometimes rightly – of applicants who can't find anything to say about half of the course; and you should be able to justify your choice of a particular combination.

what to avoid
pretentiousness: attempting to impress, you may end up out of your league. Keep your style clear and simple.
facetiousness: it's too easy to hit the wrong note and cause irritation rather than amusement.
frantic self-advertisement: avoid phrases like 'So why English and Philosophy, then?' You are applying to an English Department, not Bartle Bogle Hegarty.
writing in note form rather than continuous prose: selectors can't ask for written work from more than a small minority of candidates, so your form has to serve as evidence of your writing ability.
shaky written English: selectors are likely to take poor spelling as evidence of carelessness, and poor sentence-construction as an indication of both problems with communication and a lack of feeling for style.
illegibility: write clearly, or use a 12-point font if you are word-processing; bear in mind that the forms are reproduced in a reduced format for admission tutors.

Figure 7.5 Southampton University's English Department offers practical advice on completing the personal statement

teachers and careers advisers. Try to explain in your own words what makes you feel enthusiastic and excited about the prospect of going to university.
- The feeling that you will both benefit from and contribute to the course. You need to have done detailed research to be able to communicate this effectively.
- The impression that your decision to apply for their course is a positive one, informed by an assessment of your own abilities, aptitudes and long-term aims.

Presentation

Applications can be handwritten, typed or word-processed. Legibility is essential and you need to remember that forms are reduced in size before being forwarded to institutions. The current layout of UCAS forms is best suited to those taking A levels; students doing other qualifications need to use a little ingenuity.

- GNVQ and BTEC applicants must list all units taken. These should not be abbreviated or squashed into one line. Take the space you need to make the information clear and legible.
- You can use some of section 7A space for 7B and vice versa, but be sure to clearly label this.
- Mature students can use sections 7A and 7B as free space.
- No attachments should be sent with the form, but mature students and applicants with non-standard entry qualifications may wish to send a CV and explanatory letter directly to institutions they have chosen.

GNVQ applicants

Acceptance of Advanced GNVQ qualifications for degree courses is increasing.

- In 1998, 95 per cent of GNVQ applicants received one or more offers.
- Of the 40,000 plus higher education courses, fewer than 700 do not recognize GNVQs.

It is important that you do not waste any of your six places on any course that will not consider you. Check this quickly using the UCAS course search (see Figure 7.6).

The initial course search (see Chapter 2) allows you to stipulate GNVQ qualifications as one of your search criteria. In some cases, additional units or specific A levels are required. Many applicants with Advanced GNVQ qualifications apply for courses in the same vocational area as their current study, but some courses accept applicants from a range of GNVQ backgrounds. Entry requirements and restrictions are always made clear in paper and Web-based prospectuses.

GNVQ optional and additional units vary between colleges and students. To help admissions staff understand the compo-

```
Course details ...

Institution Name: Univ Of West Of England, Bristol

Course Name: BA Accounting and Health Science

Course Entrance Requirements:
  GNVQ:  Merit in GNVQ required
```

Figure 7.6   A UCAS result for GNVQ entry requirements

sition of your qualifications, list all the units individually and indicate whether or not they are mandatory, core or additional. UCAS gives detailed guidance on its web site and includes a sample listing of GNVQ units.

You should use part of your personal statement to explain the reason for opting for GNVQ study rather than A levels. Show how it has helped you choose your higher education courses and prepared you for self-directed study at a higher level. Some selectors worry that GNVQs are not as academically demanding as A levels. Make sure your personal statement reassures them that you are a fluent and able communicator. Highlight the other skills and opportunities GNVQs have given you, such as the ability to:

- work in teams;
- meet deadlines;
- give oral presentations;
- benefit from placement experiences.

Applications for popular courses

Some courses consistently have more applicants than places. The most oversubscribed areas are probably medicine and dentistry. The Council of Deans of UK Medical Schools recommends that no more than five UCAS choices should be used for either medical or dental courses. The remaining choice can be used for an alternative course without prejudice to your application. Other subjects – notably professions allied to medicine, such as physiotherapy, and speech therapy – should be treated in the same way. As the new financial arrangements mean that students on Health Department-funded courses are substantially better off than those on DfEE-funded courses (see Chapter 5), pressure on places may increase.

In addition to these courses, there are many others for which there is severe competition. It's usually possible to get the ratio of applicants to places from departmental Web sites or prospectus pages. Try to make sure that you apply to some departments where courses are not regularly oversubscribed. Take the popularity of a course into account when deciding which to keep as your insurance offer. Popular courses are less likely to accept applicants with grades that fall short of those stipulated in the original offer.

Where you have to select an alternative because of the popularity of your first-choice subject, make sure you'd be happy doing it. You can't go through life thinking you ended up with the second-best option.

The reference

Bear in mind that once you have completed the form, your referee needs time to write their comments. Some application systems require one, while others ask for two references. In all cases, an academic reference is essential. For the UCAS system, references can be confidential or discussed with the applicant. Your referee is asked to indicate which type of reference they are providing. Even if the reference is confidential, you can discuss it in broad terms with the writer. You may want them to highlight certain aspects of your work and achievements or address other issues. The personal statement and reference should be complementary, with the reference providing supporting evidence for what you have written about yourself. There is guidance for referees in the UCAS booklet of instructions for schools and colleges, which is available in printed form and on the Web site (see Figure 7.7).

There is no set format or recommended structure for the reference, but selectors find it helpful if the following information about the applicant is included (although this may be different for Access or modular A levels).

- *academic achievement and potential, including predicted results or peformance;*
- *suitability for the course(s)/subject(s) applied for;*
- *factors that may have influenced or may influence performance;*
- *personal qualities, such as motivation, powers of analysis, communication skills, independence of thought;*
- *career aspirations;*
- *any health or personal circumstances relevant to the application;*
- *other interests and activities;*
- *commitments that will prevent an applicant from attending an interview.*

Figure 7.7 UCAS has valuable advice for referees, too

CLEARING

UCAS and NMAS operate clearing schemes from mid July, matching unsuccessful and late applicants with courses that have vacancies. You can use it if you don't get the grades needed for your conditional offer or if you never had an offer. UCAS clearing deals with around 100,000 applications for 50,000 places.

Students who have previously applied using the system will automatically be notified of their eligibility and the procedures. It is also used by some as a method of late application, although this is not advisable as course availability is more limited than in the main application periods. It's a bit like going for a last-minute holiday — there are some 'bargains' around, but you may end up somewhere you don't want to be or not go at all.

Some students worry that courses with last-minute availability of places are somehow inferior. This is not the case. What's available is subject to chance and often reflects the general popularity of a subject area. Figure 7.8 shows a listing of course vacancies at Dundee that incorporates course assessment findings with its clearing information in order to reassure students about the quality of the courses available through clearing.

The following courses currently have vacancies:			
Course	**Vacancies?**	**Course**	**Vacancies?**
Accountancy (Excellent)	Yes	American Studies	Yes
Anatomy (Excellent)	Yes	Architecture (Satisfactory)	Yes
Biochemistry (Excellent)	Yes	Biological Chemistry (Excellent)	Yes
Biological Sciences (Excellent)	Yes	Biology (Excellent)	Yes
Botany (Excellent)	Yes	Business Economics and Marketing (Satisfactory)	Yes
Cell Biology (Excellent)	Yes	Chemistry (Satisfactory)	Yes
Civil Engineering (Highly Satisfactory)	Yes	Computing - Applied (Satisfactory)	Yes
Computing and Cognitive Science	Yes	Contemporary European Studies	Yes
Design (Excellent)	No	Dentistry (Highly Satisfactory)	No
Digital Microelectronics (Satisfactory)	Yes	Ecology (Excellent)	Yes

Figure 7.8   Many 'excellent' courses have last-minute vacancies

One of the notable features of clearing is that entry requirements are often considerably relaxed, but not all courses or institutions have vacancies. You can apply for any course with vacancies at this stage and don't have to go for subjects previously selected. You are only eligible for UCAS clearing if you:

● are holding no offers from your initial application and have not withdrawn from the UCAS scheme;
● were unsuccessful at confirmation because you failed to meet the conditions of your offers;
● decline a confirmed offer for an HND course and are holding no offers;
● decline or fail to respond to a confirmed offer of a changed course and are holding no offers.

If you are eligible for clearing, UCAS will automatically send you a clearing entry form (CEF). It posts detailed information on its web site in August.

As speed of communication is of prime importance during this frenzied period, the Web is a tremendous tool. UCAS has a regularly updated vacancy database and many universities create special clearing pages (see Figure 7.9). Some even allow you to complete and submit clearing entry forms on-line. The NISS web site (see Chapter 2) provides links to the clearing pages of all universities during this period. This has had the

Vacancies for clearing applications

Admission Requirements:

- The A level points quoted here are a guide - admissions tutors will use their judgement in deciding whether or not they will make an offer to a particular applicant
- Applications from those with non-A-level qualifications are welcomed and admissions tutors will advise in these cases
- Anyone wishing to study a science or engineering degree but with disappointing or unsuitable results should consider our Science and Engineering Foundation Studies programme
- if the points guide is active, follow it to find out more about specific admission requirements

Updated on **Thursday 20 August 1998**

Building Services Engineering	K240	16 A level points	Dr Dennis Loveday, 01509 222635 d.l.loveday@lboro.ac.uk	Department of Civil and Building Engineering
Business Studies (Based at Peterborough)	N100:P	18 A level points	Dr John Calvert, 01509 222497, j.r.calvert@lboro.ac.uk	The Business School
Chemical Engineering	H800	16 A level points	Dr Steve Tarleton, 01509 222535, e.s.tarleton@lboro.ac.uk	Department of Chemical Engineering

Figure 7.9 University clearing pages make it easy for you to see current vacancies and contact the right people immediately

effect of making the active clearing period very short-lived (see Figure 7.10). A level results normally come out on a Thursday and the majority of applicants are sorted out by the following Monday. Internet-based information is of real benefit to overseas applicants during this period. In theory, you could sort out any clearing business while on holiday anywhere in the world with Internet and e-mail connections, but, in practice, it's probably safer to be at home.

In addition to UCAS, the BBC has excellent practical advice for students on its education web pages (see Figure 1.7). National newspapers publish vacancies in paper and electronic form for a short period. The UCAS vacancy database remains operational until late September and individual university clearing Web sites until their vacancies have been filled.

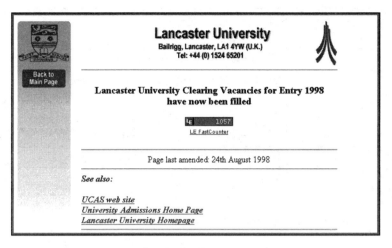

Figure 7.10 Increased speed of communication can mean that clearing is over very quickly in some universities

CHECKLIST 8: APPLICATIONS TIMETABLE

Note: If you are on a one-year course, you need to squeeze everything into a shorter timespan. Do all the things for year 1 as soon as you can and make sure you meet application deadlines.

YEAR 1	
Term 1	☑ Settle into your study and check that the subjects you have chosen suit you
Term 2	☑ Work through a self-assessment exercise
	☑ Start looking at university courses
	☑ Make a note of open day dates
	☑ Arrange a careers interview to discuss ideas
	☑ Arrange work experience
Term 3	☑ Produce a short list of suitable courses
	☑ Start in-depth investigation of alternatives

	☑ Attend a UCAS higher education convention
	☑ Investigate sponsorship
	☑ Decide whether or not you need a year off
	☑ Check the closing date of the application system you will be using
	☑ Investigate overseas opportunities
	☑ Do a basic budgeting exercise
	☑ Go to open days
	☑ Check your predicted grades
	☑ If you need to find a referee, sort that out
Summer holidays	☑ Finish course and place research
	☑ Start work on a personal statement
YEAR 2	
Term 1	☑ Complete your application form as soon as possible
	☑ Discuss your reference with the person writing it
	☑ Aim to send your completed form in by half term for systems with a December closing date
Term 2	☑ Relax and wait for offers to come back
	☑ Familiarize yourself with clearing procedures and techniques just in case

Figure 7.11   Start your planning early

The main piece of advice to keep in mind is to start planning your application early. Use the above checklist to help you do this.

———————— SITES WORTH SEEING ————————

BBC Education – Student Choice
http://www.bbc.co.uk/education/choice
This site provides a thorough guide to all aspects of clearing. The helpline is only available for a limited period, but the information remains on the site all year (see Figure 1.7).

Nurses and Midwives Admissions Service (NMAS)
http://www.nmas.ac.uk
Gives an overview of diploma courses in England with links to the university departments and information on course vacancies. An application pack can be ordered online.

Nursing Board for Scotland (NBS)
http://www.nbs.org.uk
The centralized application system, CATCH, is run by the NBS and covers all pre-registration nursing diploma courses in Scotland and links to the institutions providing them. CATCH application packs can be ordered on-line.

Nursing Board for Wales (NBW)
http://www.nbw.org.uk
Information on applying for nursing degrees and diplomas in Wales can be found here. There is no centralized application system, but you can find links to courses and check the Welsh bursary situation (see Chapter 5).

University Central Admissions Service (UCAS)
http://www.ucas.ac.uk
The course search section gives access to a comprehensive, up-to-date listing of all undergraduate degree, diploma and HND courses in the UK (see Figures 2.5–2.7). The advice section (see Figure 7.1) provides help and information on making applications.

There are plans to change the university application period so it operates after results are published. This site is the best source of information on such developments.

International Students

8

If you are an overseas student thinking of coming to study in the UK, you need to do exactly the same research as a home student. This chapter deals with the extra questions you need to ask and find answers to.

- Initial considerations
- Support services
- The costs of study in the UK
- Other considerations
- Distance learning
- Sites worth seeing

INITIAL CONSIDERATIONS

Before doing detailed research on universities and courses, check the following:

- the standard of spoken and written English required;
- the acceptability of your qualifications for the courses you are interested in;
- recognition of British degrees for professional purposes in your own country;
- immigration requirements.

The standard of spoken and written English required

All universities will require evidence that your written and spoken English will enable you to cope with study. That evidence is usually provided by your passing an English language examination. A comprehensive list can be found in the English Language Centre section of the British Council's 'Virtual Campus'. You will also find guidelines for choosing a suitable course if you need to improve your language skills.

The normal minimum language requirement for any higher education course in the UK is one of the following:

- GCSE in English language, grade C;
- an IELTS score between 5.5 and 6.5 (see Figure 8.1);
- Cambridge Proficiency in English, pass;
- NEAB University Entrance Test in English, pass.

ABOUT IELTS

- **IELTS** is a comprehensive list of English language proficiency designed to assess the ability of non-native speakers of English who itend to study or train in the medium of English.
- **IELTS** tests the complete range of English language skills which will commonly be encountered by students when studying or training in the medium of English. All candidates take the same Listening and Speaking Modules. There is an option of either Academic or General Trainning Reading and Writing Modules. Academic is suitable for candidates planning to undertake higher education study. General Training is suitable for candidates planning to undertake non academic training or work experience, or for immigration purposes.
- **IELTS** is accepted by most Australian, British, Canadian and New Zealand academic institutions. American academic institutions are increasingly accepting IELTS for admissions purposes.
- **IELTS** is accepted by many professional organisations including the New Zealand Immigration Service, the Australian Department of Immigration and Multicultural Affairs, the Australian Medical Council, the UK General Medical Council and the UK Ministry of Defence.
- **IELTS** is jointly managed by **The University of Cambridge Local Examinations Syndicate (UCLES), The British Council and IDP Education Australia: IELTS Australia.**

Figure 8.1 The IELTS site shows where you can sit these tests and has practice papers

As each university sets its own standards, you need to check specific requirements. Most run pre-sessional courses in English for academic purposes, designed to improve your language skills to meet the demands of academic study. Details can be found in the international section of university Web sites.

Entry requirements

If you wish to gain an overview of how your qualifications relate to UK higher education entry requirements, contact your local British Council office. The staff there will have experience of students from your country coming to study in the UK and will advise you on qualification requirements. The Council's Web pages for your country will have this information and contact details so you can seek further advice.

The best way to check how your achievements will be regarded is to ask the university directly. Many make the information you need available on their Web pages (see Figure 8.2) or by providing details of who you can contact to answer your questions.

Recognition of British degrees in your own country

The Department for Education and Employment (DfEE) produces a list of institutions legally authorized to award a UK degree entitled *Recognised degree courses in the United Kingdom*. Anyone claiming to award a UK degree and not appearing on this list is guilty of a criminal offence. If a degree is validated by a non-British institution, it is within the law, but will not be recognized as a British qualification, even if study took place in Britain. This list is available in British Council offices.

The Network of National Academic Recognition Centres (NARIC) works to improve academic recognition of diplomas and periods of study in the member states of the EU and the EEA. Each country has a national centre, which can provide authoritative advice and information. EU students can find information on comparability of qualifications on:

OMAN
RECOGNITION OF OMANI QUALIFICATIONS

Holders of the **Thanawiya amma** (Secondary School Leaving Certificate) may be considered for entry to the Foundation/Access/Bridging courses in the Faculties of Pure Science and Engineering.

Diploma holders from **Oman Technical Industrial College** (OTIC) may be considered for direct entry to first degree courses or Foundation/Access/Bridging courses in the Faculties of Pure Science and Engineering – where appropriate.

Holders of the **International Baccalaureate Diploma** with 28–32 points will be considered for direct admission to first degree programmes.

Holders of **'A' levels** obtained in Oman will be considered for direct admission to first degree programmes.

Details of the required **'A' level** subjects for each course and the grades required, can be found in the Undergraduate Prospectus.

Holders of a good **Bachelor** degree from Sultan Qaboos University may be considered for graduate study. This will normally be a postgraduate diploma and taught **Masters** degree.

Because of the variation in standards of secondary and higher education students should include full information regarding all their educational qualifications. Students unsure about the acceptability of their qualifications should write, for advice, to the local British Council office or the appropriate University Admissions Office, with full details of their educational background.

INTERNATIONAL STUDENTS IN SHEFFIELD 1997/98

Underdergraudate = 1230   Graduate = 1032   Total = 2262

Figure 8.2   Sheffield University gives qualification overviews for most countries

- the Citizens EU site (see Figure 8.3 and Sites worth seeing section at the end of this chapter for the address) – use it to investigate equivalence and download relevant material;
- the Europa Database (also listed in the Sites worth seeing section) – use it to find your local NARIC office.

Immigration requirements

To be regarded as a student for immigration purposes, you have to satisfy Home Office criteria. Details are on its Web site

☐ National education systems	
☐ Training and mobility of researchers	To look at the factsheets you have selected,
☐ Right of Residence	click "view", they can then be printed using the "print" button on your browser.
☐ Recognition of diplomas: Paramedical professions	VIEW
☐ Recognition of diplomas: Teachers	
☐ Recognition of diplomas: The General System	
☐ Recognition of diplomas: Engineers	
☐ Recognition of diplomas: Lawyers	
☐ Recognition of diplomas: General and Specialists Docters	
☐ Recognition of diplomas: Pharmacists	
☐ Recognition of diplomas: Dentists	
☐ Recognition of diplomas: Midwives	
☐ Recognition of diplomas: Veterinarian	

Figure 8.3 Visiting the Citizens EU site is a quick way to check the comparability of qualifications across Europe

(see Figure 8.4), including sections for dependants, student nurses and postgraduate students.

If you are from outside the EU, you may need a visa for entry to the UK. The Foreign and Commonwealth Office Web site (see Figure 8.5) provides detailed information on requirements. Its site has a comprehensive range of guidance leaflets and all the forms you need can be downloaded. The British Council office in your country will also be able to give guidance on immigration matters.

University applications

International applicants use the same admissions services as home students. These are explained in Chapter 7. All have information for overseas students on their Web sites, and application packs can be ordered electronically. All institutions in these central application systems offer courses that are validated by universities recognized by the government.

PART 3: PERSONS SEEKING TO ENTER OR REMAIN IN THE
UNITED KINGDOM FOR STUDIES

STUDENTS

Requirements for leave to enter as a student

57. The requirements to be met by a person seeking leave to enter the United
Kingdom as a student are that he:

(i) has been accepted for a course of study at:

(a) a publicly funded institution of further or higher education; or

(b) a bona fide private education institution which maintains satisfactory records
of enrolment and attendance; or

(c) an independent fee paying school outside the maintained sector; and

(ii) is able and intends to follow either:

(a) a recognised full time degree course at a publicly funded institution of
further or higher education; or

(b) a weekday full time course involving attendance at a single institution for a
minimum of 15 hours organised daytime study per week of a single subject, or
directly related subjects; or

(c) a full time course of study at an independent fee paying school; and

(iii) if under the age of 16 years

is enrolled at an independent fee paying school on a full time coure of studies
which meets the requirements of the Education Act 1944; and

(iv) intends toleave the United Kingdom at the end of his studies; and

(v) does not intend to engage in business or to take employment, except part
time or vacation work undertaken with the consent of the Secretary of State for
Employment;

(vi) is able to meet the costs of his course and accommodation and the
maintenance of himself and any dependants without taking employment or
engaging in business or having recourse to public funds.

Figure 8.4   Check for accurate, up-to-date immigration
information directly with the Home Office

SUPPORT SERVICES

The British Council

The British Council promotes all things British throughout the
world. It has a long history of providing support and information on education-related matters. There are British Council
offices in 228 towns and cities in 109 countries where you can
obtain personal guidance on studying in the UK. These
centres have comprehensive libraries of materials related to
university application. If you can't get to its offices, you'll find
a wealth of information on its well-organized Web site. It's an
excellent starting point for investigating study and life in the

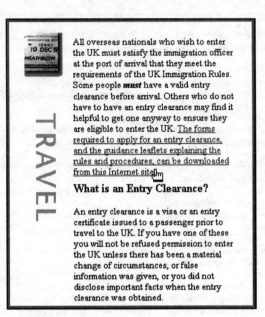

All overseas nationals who wish to enter the UK must satisfy the immigration officer at the port of arrival that they meet the requirements of the UK Immigration Rules. Some people **must** have a valid entry clearance before arrival. Others who do not have to have an entry clearance may find it helpful to get one anyway to ensure they are eligible to enter the UK. The forms required to apply for an entry clearance, and the guidance leaflets explaining the rules and procedures, can be downloaded from this Internet site.

What is an Entry Clearance?

An entry clearance is a visa or an entry certificate issued to a passenger prior to travel to the UK. If you have one of these you will not be refused permission to enter the UK unless there has been a material change of circumstances, or false information was given, or you did not disclose important facts when the entry clearance was obtained.

Figure 8.5 A quick and easy way to get all the forms you need from the FCO

UK. The 'Virtual Campus' section of the site covers all the concerns and information needs of those interested in university-level study in the UK. In addition to its main Web site, each country has its own sections.

Once you're in the UK, the British Council will continue to offer support via its international welfare service. This is a 24-hour, 7-days-a-week emergency service for immediate advice on urgent matters. Advisers based in Manchester can help with problems relating to health, budgeting, immigration, physical disability and welfare benefits.

UKCOSA – the Council for International Education

An independent organization, UKCOSA promotes educational mobility and provides support to international students and the people who work with them. It provides specialist advice on topics such as immigration, employment law, financial aid and the regulations regarding fees and grants.

University services

All universities with international students will have an international student office providing advice on all the formalities. This is your first point of contact for queries relating to accommodation, vacation work, fees and financial matters. Once you arrive, it offers a range of services to make you feel welcome and help you adjust to being a student in the UK. University Web sites have pages maintained by their international offices that show the support offered (see Figure 8.6).

THE COSTS OF STUDY IN THE UK

The costs for international students are made up of:

- the fees a university charge for tuition;
- the cost of living.

The fees charged depend on whether or not you are an EU resident.

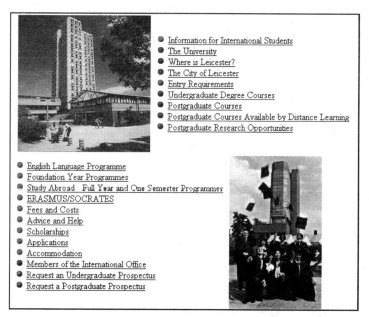

Figure 8.6   Universities use their Web sites to encourage and inform international students

Fees for EU and EEA students

EU nationals studying in the UK can get help with tuition fees from the UK authorities if they satisfy conditions similar to those for UK students. Conditions and the amount of financial help available are reviewed annually.

- Currently, the maximum fee payable by EU nationals is £1000 a year.
- Students can get means-tested help towards the cost of the fees.
- In Scotland, you may be entitled to free tuition for the final year of your course as Scottish degree courses are generally a year longer than those in the rest of the UK.

The DfEE makes the latest information on support for students available on its Web site. You can download a booklet called *Investing in the Future: Help with tuition fees for European Union (EU) students*.

It is important that you investigate this and apply for financial support before coming to the UK. Initially, you have to contact the Local Education Authority (LEA) in the area where you will be studying. The university should give you the necessary details. It is advisable to apply early as there is much paperwork.

1. The initial application form enables your LEA to decide if you are eligible for help or not.
2. If you are eligible, you will be asked to complete a means test form.
3. This will ask for details about your personal financial circumstances.
4. The means test is carried out by the DfEE, which works out how much help with fees you are entitled to.
5. It informs you and your LEA.
6. The LEA pays its share of your fees direct to your university or college. You have to pay your own contribution.
7. Each university makes its own arrangements for fee collection. Some allow you to pay in instalments.

In Scotland, your application will be dealt with by the Student Awards Agency for Scotland (SAAS) and its Web site has detailed information and guidance for EU students (see Figure 5.1). In Northern Ireland, student support is dealt with by one of the local Education and Libraries Boards. Your university or college in Northern Ireland can provide you with more details.

Fees for other international students

- Students from non-EEA countries pay the full fee.
- Higher education institutions set fees based on their costs and what they feel students will be prepared to pay.
- Fees vary considerably between institutions, by as much as £4000 a year!
- Cost reflects popularity as much as quality.
- All courses and qualifications in the UK are regulated by a system of quality inspection and assurance. See Chapter 4 for further information.

University Web sites have up-to-date information on fees. Different courses can have different fee structures and some entail extra expenditure in the form of essential equipment. It is also important to take into account the duration of the course. You can often get the same qualification from a three-year as a four-year course.

Scholarship opportunities

The number of scholarships available to foreign students is limited. Each university has information on its own schemes. Details are normally given in the international section of their site. In addition, there are Web sites such as Fundsnet, which provides free scholarship information and search facilities. The British Council's 'Virtual Campus' has scholarship details for students from the USA, Singapore and Hong Kong and lists general British government scholarships (see Figure 8.7).

What scholarships are given by the British Government?

Scholarships are given by the British Government through various schemes. The main ones are:

- Commonwealth Scholarship and Fellowship Plan (CSFP)
- British Council Fellowship Programme
- British Chevening Scholarships, funded by the FCO and DFID
- Technical Co-operation Training (TCT)
- DFID Shared Scholarship Scheme (DFIDSSS)
- The Sino-British Scholarship Scheme
- Overseas Research Students Awards Scheme (ORSAS)
- British Marshall Scholarships

Figure 8.7 There are Web sites that can help you find scholarships

Employment and study

EU students have the same right to work as UK residents. The university may be able to help you find part-time and vacation work (see Chapter 5). If you are from outside the EU and your immigration status is that of student, one condition of your stay is that you have enough money to support yourself without working or recourse to public funds (see Figure 8.4). However, many international students apply for permission to work part-time and during vacations. The stamp in your passport will tell you whether or not you may apply for permission to work and the international office at your university will be able to advise you.

The cost of living

The British Council has general information available on its Web site. Individual universities usually produce figures to show the cost of living in their area (see Figure 5.3). These are intended as a guideline. Your largest expense, excluding fees, will be accommodation. Costs vary considerably between universities, so its worth looking at this aspect during the early stages of making a choice.

Special concerns

If you have a disability, you will find well-developed services to support your study and life as a student in the UK. These are described under the heading Special concerns in other chapters in this book.

OTHER CONSIDERATIONS

Accommodation

All UK universities have student accommodation and their accommodation offices will help you find somewhere to live (see Figure 3.6). The accommodation available and comparative costs are easy to find on the Web pages for international students. It may even be possible to pay a virtual visit to the rooms you'll be living in. The main points to check, apart from price and location, are the following:

- Will you be able to use university accommodation for the whole of your course? Some universities only guarantee accommodation for first-year students.
- If you need to stay during the vacations, will the accommodation be available and what extra charges will you incur as a result?
- Is there university provision for students with families? If not, how easy is it to find suitable accommodation?

Regional differences

The UK is a country of contrasts and variety and there are universities in most regions. Differences in terms of weather, cost of living, social problems, facilities and surroundings can be considerable. You may know something of a city or region from other students or news items. You can use the Internet to get more information by accessing:

- tourist information sites;
- regional and city sites;
- Web cameras that show live pictures;
- local and national newspapers on-line;
- on-line student newspapers;
- current students – use e-mail to make contact.

Many university Web sites provide links to sites that have this information. Other sites related to this area of research are listed at the end of this chapter.

The weather

The UK's reputation for dreadful weather is perhaps a little unfair. There are considerable regional differences. In general, the west is wetter than the east; the north can be considerably colder than the south. You should budget for higher heating costs in colder parts of the country. How you regard British weather probably depends on what you're used to. If you come from a warm and dry country, then it may take some adjusting to. After a few weeks here, you'll understand why the British appear to be obsessed with the weather! To get an objective, accurate idea of what to expect, the current and historical weather data on the Met Office Web site is the best place to look.

DISTANCE LEARNING

The main provider of undergraduate distance learning courses that can be studied outside the UK is the Open University (OU). Students can study at their own pace for UK-accredited degrees in a variety of disciplines. Courses are taught via correspondence texts, video and audio tapes, TV broadcasts and the Internet. There are no formal entrance requirements, but present study areas are EU countries, plus Gibraltar, Slovenia and Switzerland. Students in Bulgaria, the

Czech Republic, Hong Kong, Hungary, Romania, Russia, Singapore and South Africa may study a selection of OU courses via partner organizations.

Most overseas students will have to pay an additional charge to cover the extra costs of services to them. Tuition fees are higher for non-EU students as they are not eligible for government subsidy. If your chosen course has a residential school, you will probably have to travel to the UK to attend it. Full details are on the OU Web site.

Details of postgraduate distance learning courses offered by other UK universities can be obtained from the British Council. The OU maintains an excellent database of distance learning opportunities at all levels and from providers world-wide.

CHECKLIST 9: OVERSEAS STUDENTS CHECKLIST
Web resources to use
University:
Course:
Language requirements: *International students' pages* *Departmental pages* *IELTS* *British Council*
Pre-sessional course available: *International students' pages*
Entry requirements: *International students' pages* *Departmental pages* *Direct e-mail contact*

Recognition of UK qualification in your country:
British Council
Professional bodies' Web sites
NARIC
Citizens EU

Immigration formalities:
Home Office
Foreign and Commonwealth Office
British Council
UKCOSA

Course and place research:
(Also complete Checklist 3, page 73)
University Web sites
Tourist information sites
Met Office
Newspapers
Student organizations
Map sites
Web cameras

Quality:
(Also complete Checklist 4, page 89)
Funding council sites
The Times' league tables
Red Mole

Costs:
(Also complete Checklist 5, page 113)
University Web sites
DfEE

Scholarships:
British Council
Fundsnet

Accommodation details:
Accommodation services pages

Overseas students should also complete the other checklists in this book.

──────── SITES WORTH SEEING ────────

In addition to using the sites described below, international students need to go through the same processes of investigating and applying for courses as home students. Details of Web sites to help with this are given in this section in the appropriate chapters.

Initial considerations

Citizens EU
http://citizens.eu.int
This is a well-organized site that allows you to enter your country of origin and the country you want to investigate. There is information on work and education opportunities for each member state. You'll find detailed information on comparability of professional qualifications and the facility to order or download related booklets (see Figure 8.3).

Europa Database
http://europa.eu.int
This is a huge resource with information on all the schemes that promote student mobility in Europe.

Foreign and Commonwealth Office
http://www.fco.gov.uk
The visa information pages allow you to download all the necessary leaflets and forms (see Figure 8.5). You will need Adobe Acrobat Reader to view these files. There is a link to the site from which this can be downloaded for free. The address is:

http://www.adobe.com/prodindex/acrobat/
download.html

You can personalize the FCO site to highlight subjects of your choice or to receive automatic e-mail notification of news, texts or travel advice notices.

Home Office
http://www.homeoffice.gov.uk/ind/contents.htm
Detailed up-to-date information on immigration law can be found here (see Figure 8.4).

International English Language Testing System (IELTS)
http://www.ielts.org
Comprehensive test of your English language proficiency (see Figure 8.1).

NARIC
http://europa.eu.int/en/comm/dg22/socrates/agenar.html
Look here for a full listing of all EU NARIC contacts.

Support services

British Council Worldwide
http://www.britcoun.org
The main site has links to British Council offices worldwide. It has a wealth of information on all aspects of British life. There is a substantial amount of reference material related to study in the UK. The 'Virtual Campus' (see Figure 8.7) is a self-contained section for overseas students and covers everything you need. It can be accessed from the main site or directly:

http://www.britcoun.org/eis/campus.htm

UKCOSA – the Council for International Education
http://www.ukcosa.org.uk
A specialist advice service is offered here on international education and student mobility. UKCOSA will deal with enquiries by e-mail. To do this, use the following address:

enquiries@ukcosa.org.uk

sites worth seeing

The cost of study

DfEE – Higher Education Student Support
http://www.open.dfee.uk/support/index.htm
The DfEE provides regularly updated information on financial support for students in higher education at this site. There are pages specifically for EU students coming to the UK.

Fundsnet
http://www.fundsnetservices.com
This is a database of links to charities and grant-making bodies worldwide. See Chapter 5.

Other considerations

E&P Directory of Online Newspapers
http://www.mediainfo.com/emedia

Kidon Media Link
http://www.dds.nl/~kidon/media-link/papers.shtml
Find and read local and national newspapers using one of the above. Both sites have listings of, and links to, all the world's major newspapers.

Student newspapers
http://www.nus.org.uk/studentm.html
Reading the student newspaper for the university you are going to can give real insights. The NUS provides links to all of them.

UK Multimap
http://www.multimap.com
This site has address-searching and street map facilities for the UK. Currently street maps are only available for Greater London, but there is an excellent road atlas for the whole of mainland Britain.

UK Meteorological Office

http://www.meto.gov.uk

Find out for yourself what British weather is really like. There are current and historical details here.

Visit Britain

http://www.visitbritain.com

Investigate all the things you can do when you're not studying. This site is run by the British Tourist Authority. It covers most things visitors to the UK need to know and includes 'Britain for Walkers' and 'Britain for Cyclists', which are databases of suggested itineraries. There are lots of wonderful pictures, though these make it slow to load.

Web cameras

http://www.cybertour.com
http://www.windows2000.com

Indexes for, and reviews of a huge range of live cameras across the world can be found at these sites.

Distance learning

Open University

http://www.open.ac.uk

Detailed information for prospective students can be found here, including information on courses delivered via the Internet.

Open University International Centre for Distance Learning

http://www-icdl.open.ac.uk

Look here for information on institutions worldwide that offer distance learning programmes. You can search for a specific course, institution, or subject.

Appendix: Effective Internet Use at School, College or Home

- The basics
- Understanding your browser
- Accessibility for disabled users
- Coping with URLs
- Effective searching
- Getting the most from e-mail
- Using free services
- Understanding e-mail addresses
- Making use of mailing lists and newsletters
- Getting the best from newsgroups
- Using the Internet at home
- Understanding and evaluating the costs
- Online charges
- Hints and tips for cost-effective Internet use
- Sites worth seeing

THE BASICS

If you're contemplating higher education, you're going to have to learn to love your computer. It's normal for tutors to ask for your work to be word-processed and much reference material is accessed through internal university networks or the Internet. Computer literacy is taken for granted, just as much as ordinary literacy was a generation ago. Today's undergraduates are expected to have well-developed information and communications technology skills and to keep them updated.

When you're using the Internet at school or college, all the costs and technical problems are taken care of by someone else. All you have to concern yourself with is using your time effectively and being able to find the information you want. The first part of this Appendix will help you do that. If you're an experienced user, it will help you develop more efficient techniques. If you'd rather not touch a computer, it will give you the know-how and confidence to have a go.

You may want to have Internet access at home, so understanding costs is important. The second part of the Appendix looks at how to keep costs down and develop good browsing habits that will save you time and money. You also need to make sure that you have an up-to-date virus checker to protect your computer against damaging files from the Internet.

What the Internet is

- A network of computers linked by the telephone system.
- A way of moving information around the world quickly and efficiently.
- A tool for sharing information, promoting understanding and free speech, encouraging learning and exchanging ideas.

The Internet has already had a profound effect on the way we learn, conduct research and communicate, and that influence is going to increase. Its potential benefits are enormous. No matter where you live, you have access to information from all parts of the world on all subjects. Whatever you are researching, you will find an unsurpassable store of information that can be accessed easily, cheaply and at any time of the day or night. Like many computer applications, it's simple to use once you've mastered a few techniques.

The World Wide Web

The Web is the glossy multimedia magazine component of the Internet, with attractively presented information on every subject from all over the world. The information is linked in a way that gives it a web-like structure – that is, by following links, you go to related information. You can look at things in greater depth and make connections you might not otherwise have thought of, but this can also mean that you end up going round in circles, feeling trapped and frustrated. In theory, you can find everything you would ever want with the click of a mouse. In practice, you need to spend a little time developing efficient search techniques in order to utilize the tremendous potential it offers.

Web sites and Web pages

The World Wide Web contains millions of Web sites. A web site is a collection of documents known as Web pages that have been put together by a person or organization. Each page has links that take you to related information. This could be to another page on the same site or to another site in a different part of the world. Links can be shown as coloured, underlined text or a picture. Clicking on a link takes you to the new site or page.

Skills needed

You don't need to know much about computers to use the Web. Basic keyboarding skills are enough as the screens you work with are similar to those on word processors. What you do need to learn is how to search effectively, evaluate what you find and avoid being swamped by irrelevant material.

UNDERSTANDING YOUR BROWSER

Browser software

You explore the Web using a browser. It helps you move and browse through interconnected documents that can come from anywhere in the world. Many new computers have browsers included as part of their start-up software. Once you have an Internet connection, you can download the browser software of your choice from the Web.

Appendix

Navigator or Explorer?

The main browsers are Netscape Navigator and Internet Explorer. The basic versions of both are free, and you may wish to compare them and see which you prefer. They have slightly different icons and commands, but perform the same functions and are similar in appearance. Like everything else associated with the Internet, browsers are continually being upgraded. If you want to keep up with developments, look at:

```
http://www.browsers.com
```

It is not necessary to have the most up-to-date browser. In some cases, an older computer may not be powerful enough to run the latest browser software.

Understanding Web pages

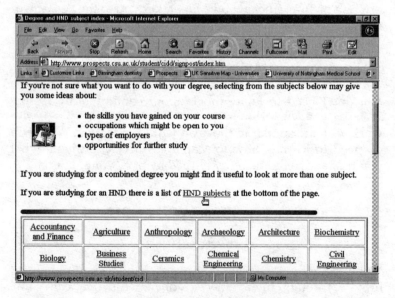

Figure A.1   A typical Web page viewed using Internet Explorer 4

Appendix

The layout of a Web page (see Figure A.1) is similar to that of most word-processed documents:

- the status bar lets you know where a link will take you and the speed of current transmission or file size;
- the progress bar fills as a transmission is being made;
- the pointer moves round the page – use it to click on words, images or the scroll bar;
- the pointer changes from an arrow to a hand when it is placed over a link;
- links are usually coloured, underlined text or a picture.

Using the commands

You can look at browser software without being online. Spending time off-line, getting used to the layout and functions of your browser, costs nothing. In addition, there are certain things – such as sorting out favourites or composing e-mail – that you can do off-line. Then, when you go online, you will be familiar with the common commands and able to work quickly.

The commands that allow you to change settings and move around the Web are at the top of the screen. Figure A.2 shows the standard settings for Internet Explorer 4. On newer browsers, commands can be customized to include functions you use frequently.

The title bar has the name of the page you are viewing and the 'minimize', 'restore' and 'close' buttons.

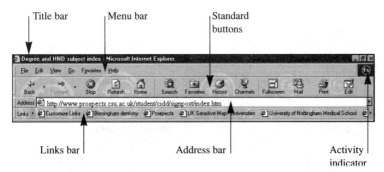

Figure A.2 Browser commands and menus

The commands included in the menu bar enable you to carry out a range of functions, such as:

- changing the appearance of your screen;
- preventing the automatic loading of images;
- printing;
- copying and pasting text;
- searching for a specific word in the displayed document.

The toolbar provides quick links to popular commands from the menu bar. The commands are activated by a single click of the mouse. When their use is not available to you, the icons are 'greyed out' (see the 'forward' button in Figure A.2). Here, the toolbar is in picture and text form, but it can also be displayed as just pictures or just text. On newer browsers, allowing your pointer to dwell on a toolbar button will display its function.

The *back* button takes you to the previous page you were viewing.

The *forward* button takes you to the next open page and can only be used after going back. Both the back and forward buttons have drop-down boxes available once pages have been viewed.

The *stop* button is useful when transfers are taking too long and you wish to terminate a connection. Keep an eye on the status bar at the bottom of the screen to see the progress of transmissions. Your modem may have the potential to operate at up to 56kbps, but information is sometimes received at less than one per cent of this speed.

The *refresh* button reloads your current page. This is useful if a transfer of information has been interrupted or corrupted or you want to update it.

The *home* button takes you to your home page. This is the first page you connect to when you access the Web. It is normally set by the ISP to take you to its site, but you can change it to a page of your choice, either on the Web or from your existing computer files.

The *search* button takes you to selected search engines.

The *favourites* button takes you directly to sites you've previously added to your favourites file.

The *history* button shows a list of recently visited sites. You can use it in a limited way for off-line browsing.

The *channels* button shows a list of sites that can be automatically updated.

The *fullscreen* button allows you to make the web page you are viewing take up most of the screen. Clicking the fullscreen icon once you are in fullscreen view restores the page to its normal size.

The *mail* button takes you to your e-mail program.

The *print* button prints the current Web page. A Web page can be several screen or paper pages long. The print dialogue box, which appears after you have clicked on this button, allows you choose whether to print specific pages or the whole document.

The *edit* button allows you to edit the Web page you are viewing.

The links bar displays links from your favourites folder. It can be customized.

The address bar gives you the location or URL of the Web page you are viewing.

The activity indicator becomes animated when data is being transmitted.

Help pages

All the software has help sections (see Figure A.3). You can print the pages that deal with relevant topics and explore the facilities your browser offers without connecting to the Internet. If you're using a public access point, explain what you are doing and ask for free time to do it. As you are accessing the computer's hard disk rather than going online, it should not incur the same charge.

ACCESSIBILITY FOR DISABLED USERS

The Internet makes it possible for everyone to communicate easily. For people with disabilities, it holds the promise of removing barriers to education and information access. New technologies can bring new barriers, but much thought and effort has been put into making the Internet accessible to disabled users. Organizations such as the Web Accessibility

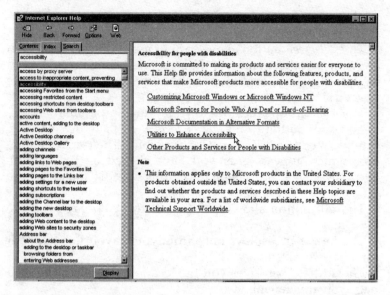

Figure A.3 You'll find answers to most questions in the help sections

Initiative address issues of Web use and disability, providing practical help and suggestions for all.

Web designers are being encouraged to develop pages that are accessible to all, including visually impaired users and those with dyslexia. The Centre for Applied Special Technology (CAST) provides a service that analyses Web page accessibility. Pages that meet their standards can display the Bobby symbol (see Figure A.4).

We have worked hard to make this site accessible to all and so we are proud to bear the *Bobby Approved* icon.

Figure A.4 Bobby-approved pages meet the browsing needs of those with disabilities

Appendix

Customizing page appearance

If the way a Web page is designed and presented makes it difficult for you to use, most browsers will allow you to customize it. Font size can be changed from the menu or tool bar. Options for changing colour settings for fonts and page background vary between browsers, but details can always be found in the help section.

With Microsoft Windows 95 and later versions, there is an accessibility option (see Figure A.5) in the control panel. It allows you to select settings that apply to all the programs you have, and enables you to customize how you view pages and use keyboard commands.

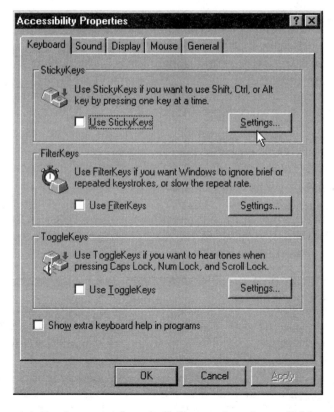

Figure A.5 A range of accessibility options is available

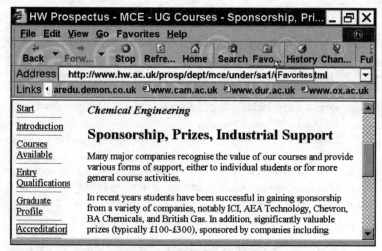

Figure A.6   A high-contrast black on white page

The 'display' tab has the option for a high-contrast setting. You can choose the colour combination and when you apply it everything increases in size, including font, buttons and dialogue boxes (see Figure A.6).

COPING WITH URLs

The World Wide Web is made up of a huge number of sites. Each site and each page has its own unique address, known as a Uniform Resource Locator (URL). In order to visit a site, you need to enter its URL in the address bar. There are various ways to do this:

- you can type the URL directly into the address bar and then press enter;
- if you arrive at a page or site via a hypertext link, you may not know its URL, but will see it displayed in the address bar – add those that are useful to your favourites file so that you can access them again easily;
- copy links to your favourites file off-line by right clicking on them from any document, then, when you select a favourite, the URL will automatically be transferred to the address bar.

An efficiently organized favourites file makes an enormous difference to effective use of the Web. Time spent doing this is easily repaid later. Details relating to organizing a favourites file will be in the browser's help pages.

The importance of accuracy

URLs are like phone numbers – they only work if you get them exactly right. It is worth taking time to understand how they are made up. Getting error messages saying the URL you've just typed in doesn't exist is frustrating and wastes time. The accuracy needed extends to whether you use upper or lower case letters, where you put your full stops and what sort of slash or dash you use. At its simplest, a URL looks something like this:

```
http://www.ucas.ac.uk
```

What it all means
- **http**   Stands for Hypertext Transfer Protocol. It is always followed by :// It tells your browser what type of document you want. For normal Web documents, you do not need to enter it as part of the address — the browser assumes that if you enter nothing, http:// should be there. Other commonly used protocols are ftp:// and news:// Secure sites start with https:// (see Figure 1.3).
- **www.ucas.**   This is known as the 'domain name' and tells you the name of the server and company/organization/individual you are connecting to.
- **ac.**   Tells you what sort of organization it is. Commonly used ones are:

ac.	=	academic institution in the UK only. Elsewhere its denoted by edu
co.	=	commercial company in the UK
com.	=	commercial company elsewhere and increasingly in the UK
gov.	=	governmental organization
org.	=	other types of organization
sch.	=	school site
net.	=	Internet service provider

● **uk**   This tells you in which country the site originates. Every country has its own code – fr = France; is = Iceland; ie = Ireland; za = South Africa; pl = Poland. American Web sites do not normally use a country code. Resist the temptation to put a full stop at the end of a URL — there never is one!

The basic URL will generally take you to the home page of a Web site. This provides content lists or site maps to help you find your way around the site.

Finding specific files

URLs that extend beyond the country code are the addresses of specific pages or files. They are separated from the main body of the URL by a / (forward slash). For example:

```
http://www.ucas.ac.uk/getting/prospect/
appform/internat/index.html
```

is a page that deals with UCAS applications for international students.

Specific files like these can change. If a URL is taking you to a current piece of information, that file may disappear when information is updated and trying to reach it will result in an error message. If this happens, go to the address bar and delete back as far as the first forward slash. Using the example above, that would be to:

```
http://www.ucas.ac.uk
```

which is the site's home page. You can then use the search facility to find the page you need.

Mistakes are often made when URLs are typed and sites do move and disappear. It can be frustrating when you've read about a site that looks like it will answer your questions and then you can't find it. If the site has moved, there may be a message and a hypertext link that will take you to the new address. If not, you should be able to find a site's new location by searching for the site name or the topic it deals with using a search engine or Web directory.

EFFECTIVE SEARCHING

Unlike other libraries of information, there is no single classification system on the Web. It would be impossible to make use of this huge body of information without some index. Search engines, directories and meta-searchers act as index and contents pages for Web information. They are powerful tools that can help you find what you want. Many have enthusiastic-sounding names, such as Yahoo!, Yell and Excite, and, indeed, they do behave in an enthusiastic manner – quickly fetching lots of interesting things for you to look at. This can cause problems, though. You can get hundreds, thousands, even millions, of documents if your search is too general and none if it's too specific. Searches only take a few seconds to perform, even if they return a huge number of matches.

Search engines, directories and meta-searchers

- **Search engines**   Also called 'spiders' or 'crawlers', search engines run automatically and visit Web sites on the Internet in order to catalogue them. This means that they are constantly updating their content. They search on word match rather than context and this results in a lot of irrelevant documents. Advanced searching techniques can help overcome this.
- **Directories**   These are compiled by humans. Sites are submitted by their authors and assigned an appropriate category. This means they often produce more relevant results than search engines, but are sometimes less comprehensive.
- **Meta-search engine**   If you are having difficulty finding information on a subject, you could try one of these. They send your query to several search engines and directories at once.
- **Geographically specific resources**   These concentrate on a particular area of the world. Large directories, such as Yahoo!, have country-specific sections and most countries have search tools that are specific to them. For example, there are Channel Hong Kong (http://www.chkg.com) and Euroferret (http://www.euroferret.com — see Figure A.7).

Figure A.7 Regional search tools can produce more relevant results

- **Subject gateways** These are often compiled and maintained by universities and offer access to subject expertise worldwide. They are very detailed, comprehensive and accurate (see Chapter 2).

There will be links to several large search engines via the 'search' button on your browser. Alternatively, you can use one of your choice by typing its URL into the address bar. In addition to general search tools, a number of search engines and directories concentrate on academic material.

Successful searching

Finding the right search tool for your query is essential. For academic matters, 'The Academic Directory' shown in Figure A.8 or subject gateways described in Chapter 2 will enable you to focus on relevant material. In addition to engines that search sections of, or the whole, Web, many sites have an internal search facility.

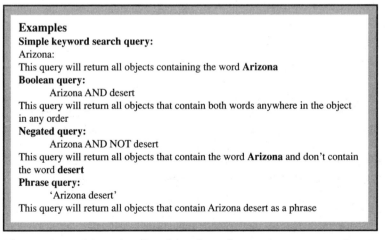

Figure A.8 HENSA Unix provides a very focused tool and links to similar projects

> **Examples**
> **Simple keyword search query:**
> Arizona:
> This query will return all objects containing the word **Arizona**
> **Boolean query:**
>   Arizona AND desert
> This query will return all objects that contain both words anywhere in the object in any order
> **Negated query:**
>   Arizona AND NOT desert
> This query will return all objects that contain the word **Arizona** and don't contain the word **desert**
> **Phrase query:**
>   'Arizona desert'
> This query will return all objects that contain Arizona desert as a phrase

Figure A.9 It's quite simple to broaden or narrow searches

If you're getting too many or too few matches, take time to look at the help section of the search engine and experiment with techniques suggested. Each has different options for refining a search; all have extensive help sections. Figure A.9 is from the help section of 'The Academic Directory'.

GETTING THE MOST FROM E-MAIL

This is the most widely used tool on the Internet. As well as being a cheap and efficient way of communicating, e-mail enables you to 'observe' or participate in group discussions via mailing lists. If you're at school or college, you may be given an individual e-mail address. If you have your own connection, it will normally include e-mail. In addition, there are lots of services that offer free Web-based e-mail.

How it works

Messages are stored in a personal postbox and can be collected at any time. In most cases, messages can be composed off-line, stored and sent together during cheap rate for phone calls. How long they take to transmit depends on their length, but five short messages to five different countries can easily be sent in under a minute.

Advantages

- You can send messages, attach pictures, documents and even sounds to anyone else who has an e-mail address.
- It is easy to send copies of the same message to different people.
- There is no need to worry about time zones – an e-mail sent in the middle of the night doesn't wake anyone.
- Material arrives in pristine condition.
- Messages and attachments can be printed or stored on a computer.
- It costs the same to send whatever the destination.
- Where an e-mail can't be delivered, it is generally returned to the sender with an explanation of the problem.

Disadvantages

- You have to pay to look at your e-mail because you go on-line to receive it.
- It is not always totally reliable. Mail can disappear completely, pretty much like conventional mail, although this only happens rarely.
- Messages are usually transferred quickly, but graphics can take a long time. You can instruct your browser not to accept e-mails above a certain size.

Subject lines

What your recipient initially sees on their screen is your name and the subject matter of your message. It is important to fill in the subject line so that there is some indication of what you are writing about. If that person gets a lot of unsolicited mail, then they may ignore messages with no subject line.

USING FREE SERVICES

e-mail

If you don't have an Internet account or frequently change providers, there are several companies who offer free e-mail accounts. The pages you access to use e-mail have adverts and the company gets its revenue from them. It is normally possible to access your free e-mail account from any computer with an Internet connection, using a name and password unique to you.

Forwarding services

Some providers of free e-mail addresses act as forwarders as well. This means that they automatically send on mail from your free address to any e-mail address you nominate. The result is that you can have one e-mail address that will not change, regardless of how many times you change provider.

You could set one up to forward to your school postbox then to a university or personal postbox when you move on.

Some Internet service providers (ISPs), schools and universities block all e-mail from certain free provider addresses, such as Hotmail, because it generates a lot of junk mail. If you have a free account, send a few test e-mails to friends to see if they get through.

UNDERSTANDING E-MAIL ADDRESSES

A typical address will look like this:

```
poor.student@free-mail.com
irene@serviceprovider.net
ik@adviser.co.uk
```

They are similar to URLs and require the same attention to accuracy. The first part of the address is the name you choose for yourself. It may not always be your first name or initials because once a name has been allocated, it cannot be used by anyone else. If the name you want has been taken, you have to use a certain amount of imagination and ingenuity in choosing one to represent you. Your name is always followed by @ (at). The next part shows who your account is with and follows the same conventions as URLs.

It is easy to set up different addresses for different purposes. Many ISPs give you more than one address and there is no limit to the number of free ones you can use. If you're going to be using e-mail to communicate with universities and employers, think of the impression you want to create. partyanimal@anytime.com may not go down as well with them as it does with your friends.

MAKING USE OF MAILING LISTS AND NEWSLETTERS

Mailing lists provide a forum for discussion on a huge range of topics. If you join a mailing list, you will have the discussion posted to you as e-mails. This can mean hundreds of items a day!

Appendix

Joining a mailing list

You join a mailing list by 'subscribing' to it, but subscription is free. You will either fill in a form on a Web site (this often asks for no more than your e-mail address) or send an e-mail to the relevant address with a message such as subscribe followed by the name of the list you wish to receive.

The first thing you receive is a confirmation of your subscription and details of how to cancel or 'unsubscribe'. It's important to keep these details so that if you no longer want that information, you can stop it arriving. It's also a good idea to unsubscribe to mailing lists if you're going to be away for some time – otherwise you'll come back to thousands of messages clogging up your postbox. It's a bit like remembering to cancel the milk and just as necessary!

Finding lists

All UK academic mailing lists can be found via Mailbase (see Figure A.10). There are also directories of general mailing lists, such as The Liszt, where you can search for any related to your interests.

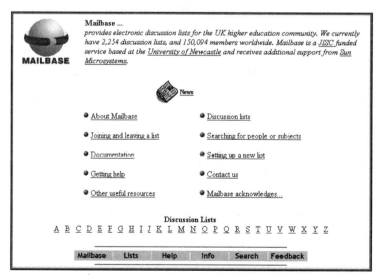

Figure A.10 Observe or join in on discussions of any academic subject

Different types of lists

Mailing lists are closed or open, moderated or unmoderated:

- closed lists just send information to you;
- open mailing lists allow you to contribute to the discussion and can be unmoderated or moderated;
- unmoderated lists automatically display all messages posted;
- moderated lists are those where someone checks the suitability of messages and decides which to include.

Moderation can be useful because it prevents irrelevant, offensive or advertising material creeping in. Most people who act as moderators of lists are unpaid and do it for the love of the subject.

e-zines and newsletters

As well as being available on the Web, many e-zines and newsletters can be subscribed to in the same way as mailing lists. Avoid the temptation to subscribe to too many lists and newsletters at once or you'll spend all your time looking at your post!

GETTING THE BEST FROM NEWSGROUPS

Newsgroups are 'places' where people with similar interests exchange views, ask questions, offer help and occasionally bicker and insult each other. There are in excess of 30,000 newsgroups, contributed to by over 40 million people. Contributors can be experts in their field or weird eccentrics. You should take the same precautions as you would with all other parts of the Internet. If you are using the Internet at school or college, you may not have access to newsgroups.

Understanding newsgroup names

Each newsgroup has a unique name made up of several parts. These give you an indication of the subject they are dealing with and help you choose appropriate ones. The first part of the name shows which category it comes into and can be prefixed by a country code. Some popular ones are:

- **alt.** alternative newsgroups, informal and unofficial sources of information;
- **biz.** commercial and business matters;
- **comp.** computer-related discussion;
- **misc.** catch-all for subjects that don't fit anywhere else;
- **sci.** scientific discussion;
- **rec.** recreational interests;
- **soc.** discussions on cultural, social and religious issues.

The second part gives you an indication of the subject they're dealing with. For example:

- alt.appalachian.literature
- biz.marketplace.international
- comp.answers
- misc.education.language.english
- rec.arts.dance
- sci.geo.geology
- soc.religion.eastern
- uk.sci.med.pharmacy

Selecting and subscribing to newsgroups

Newsgroups can be accessed via newsreading software that normally forms part of your Internet connection package. Initially, you need to be online to receive the full list of newsgroups kept by your ISP. Receiving this list takes a few minutes, but then you can look at and search it off-line. There is usually a facility to search for key words so you don't have to go through the full 30,000. The number you get access to depends on your ISP.

Subscribing and unsubscribing are fully explained in the help section of the software you are using. Once you have subscribed, new articles will be posted to you and you collect them in the same way that you collect mail. You can of course read them off-line. There may be hundreds of new articles each day for any one newsgroup, so avoid the temptation to subscribe to lots. Use the help sections of your newsreading software to find out how you can just download message titles to save time and then get the full text of messages that interest you later.

Netiquette

This refers to a loose set of 'rules' on how to behave on the Internet and applies particularly to participation in newsgroups and mailing lists. Essentially, it encourages people to behave in a considerate and intelligent manner. You'll find detailed descriptions of what should and shouldn't be done in the information that comes from your ISP. Take time to acquaint yourself with what is regarded as acceptable behaviour and what is not. The Internet gives you the potential to offend or impress millions!

Frequently asked questions (FAQs)

It's always a good idea to look at the FAQ list before you ask a question as it may have already been covered. Most newsgroups, mailing lists and even Web sites have them.

USING THE INTERNET AT HOME

Before using the Internet at home, make sure you have an up-to-date virus checker. These can be downloaded from the Internet – details about them are given at the end of this Appendix.

If you use the Internet at school or college it's easy to develop bad browsing habits! Institutions usually have dedicated lines for Internet use and pay a standard charge regardless of how much time is spent connected to the phone. These may be able to download information more efficiently than your equipment at home.

UNDERSTANDING AND EVALUATING THE COSTS

There are three main types of cost to consider in relation to using the Internet:

- buying or upgrading a computer to enable you to access the Internet;
- the subscription you pay to your ISP;
- your phone bill.

The hardware

To connect to the Internet, you need a computer, a modem and a telephone. Computers bought in the last few years generally come with all the hardware and software you need for an Internet connection. However, if you have an older computer with sufficient memory and hard disk space, you can add a modem and the necessary software to it. It is still possible to get Internet software that will run on Windows 3.1, but, increasingly, Internet software requires Windows 95 or later versions. If you don't want to spend money on a computer, but want to access the Internet outside school, there are a number of places that offer public Internet access, including:

- libraries;
- cybercafés;
- colleges and universities.

Modems

A modem is the piece of hardware that connects your computer to the phone system. New computers generally come with an internal modem, but it is possible to buy an external one to connect to your computer. The faster your modem and computer are, the quicker you will receive and send data. This minimizes time spent on-line, which usually has a cost attached to it. Modem speeds are measured in bits per second (bps). A bit is the basic unit of computer data. The more your modem can cope with each second, the better. The speed modems operate at is continually increasing. The best sources of up-to-date information on equipment are articles and adverts in the many Internet magazines. These are available on the Web as well as in paper form.

A modem can act as an answering and fax machine when linked to your computer. This is independent of the Internet and a useful extra resource. Check that any modem you're buying has these facilities.

Modem speed

The speed at which modems can work is not matched by the speed at which data is actually transferred. That depends on the volume of traffic and all the other computers and modems you are linking to. Like a telephone, a modem can be engaged and therefore prevent you accessing the information you want. A major complaint users have is the length of time it can take to receive data. This can be optimized to a certain extent.

Internet technology is changing and improving all the time. Speed of data transmission is likely to increase in the long term, but may slow down in the short term as the systems struggle to cope with ever-increasing numbers of users. You can always choose not to look at information that is taking too long to get through to you by stopping the transfer and trying again at a less busy time.

ISP charges

In September 1998, the Dixons Group launched Freeserve – a full Internet access service with no registration or subscription fees and no hourly on-line charges (see Figure A.11). It gives unlimited access to the Internet, newsgroups and e-mail facilities. Installation disks can be picked up from any of their shops.

The main differences between Freeserve and subscription services are:

- the cost of calls to the helpline – while with most providers, these are local or national call rates, for the Dixons helpline calls are charged at the premium rate of £1 a minute, but there is extensive online help and a free e-mail help service;
- its software is only for Windows 95, 98 or NT 4.0.

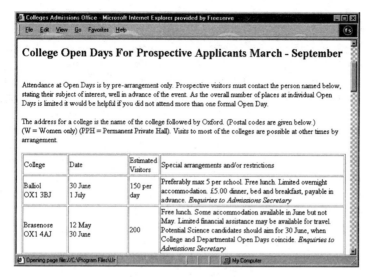

Figure A.11   There is such a thing as a free lunch!

At the product launch, Dixons' Chairman said, 'By removing monthly subscription charges we believe that Freeserve will revolutionize the Internet service market and drive up Internet use'. He was right. There are now several major ISPs competing to give away free Internet accounts.

Like many things associated with the Internet, this situation is changing rapidly and it's easy to use the Internet to keep up to date with it. Internet magazines have regular features that compare the services and charges of ISPs. It certainly pays to shop around and compare the services offered and costs or lack of them (see Figure A.14).

ONLINE CHARGES

The time you spend online connected to the Internet via your telephone always has a cost attached to it. This could be the cost of phone calls, provider charges if you have a limited hours package or the value of your own time. Time somehow changes shape once you become absorbed in what you are doing. You follow links, get interested in what's there and the ten minutes you'd intended to spend has transformed itself into three hours.

You can significantly reduce the time you spend online by always reading and printing documents offline. Any document you view is stored in the computer's memory cache for a time. The help section of your web browser software will tell you how to regulate the size and content of the cache and what its limitations are. You can open these files without being connected to the phone. With the latest browsers, there is an option to work offline on files stored in the cache or you can use the 'file, save as' command when viewing a page. This will save a document but not any graphics or links you followed. Pictures can be saved separately. Do this by clicking on an image with the right mouse button, which will bring up an option box allowing you to do a range of things with that picture.

Offline reading software

Offline browsers are widely available and make the process of looking at sites visited a lot easier. They process the cache into an index that retains the original file names and URLs and allows you to follow any links that you made while online (see Figure A.12). Images are retained within the processed web pages. This is useful if you have an older browser without an offline option or if you want to be able to search, store or organize files from your cache.

This software can be obtained as freeware or shareware downloaded from the Web. You can find details of what's available using a search engine or one of the shareware sites.

HINTS AND TIPS FOR COST-EFFECTIVE INTERNET USE

- **Check on free Internet access provision** There are now several free providers competing with Dixons and it's probable that this area will grow. Check what each offers, particularly the system requirements and any hidden costs. If you need to buy a new computer to run the free software, then it might not be quite the saving it first appears.

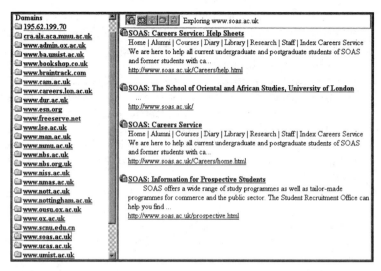

Figure A.12 Unmozify organizes and displays your cache efficiently for offline use

- **If you opt for a service with a fee, use free trials before you decide who to sign up with** There can be a significant difference between different ISPs and many offer a range of subscription packages. Restricted time is always cheaper than unlimited access and worth considering if you know you are likely to just use it for a few hours a month. If, however, you go over the agreed number of hours, the charges per extra hour can be high. Be wary of committing yourself to one provider for a long time – this is an area of rapidly changing costs and offers.

- **Investigate call discount schemes** If you pay for local calls, check whether or not your phone company has a scheme for offering discounts on frequently called numbers and add the ISP's Internet access number to it. Where a phone company is also offering Internet access, it may offer discounted calls to customers using its system. Cable companies may provide telephone services that offer some free local calls.

- **Use the Internet when it's cheap and fast** Access the Web during cheap rate for phone calls, and try to do most of your searching at times that are not busy. This varies depending where you live, but essentially it's governed by whether the largest user, the USA, is asleep or awake. At busy times, you may fail to make connections and data transfer will be slower.

- **Access sites via your favourites file** Create favourites offline so that time online is not spent typing in long URLs. Favourites (also known as bookmarks and hotlists) can be arranged in folders and moved around. Have the ones you want to visit at the top of your favourites file. Explore the facilities available for organizing your favourites offline using the help section.

- **Avoid slow-loading home pages** A site's home page is not always the best one to select as your future starting point. Many take a long time to load, while subsequent pages are usually plainer and give access to the rest of the site.

- **Stop images, sound and video clips being loaded automatically** Instruct your browser not to load these. All browsers have an option to turn automatic loading on and off – details will be in their help sections. Pages without images take less time to load. The picture is replaced by an icon that you click on to load the picture.

- **Don't try to read information on screen** Go quickly to any links that interest you – your eye will be drawn to them because they are coloured and underlined text or pictures. Watch the status bar, which tells you what's happening with your connections and data transfer. Once it says 'done' or words to that effect, it has cached the link you requested and you can go back to where you started using the 'back' button. Do the same with all the other useful links. (If you hit the back button before it's all loaded, you get a message telling you the transfer has been interrupted. You end up with an incomplete document and will need to reload.) Use offline browser software to read pages and evaluate their usefulness.

- **Print out information while offline** Read it at your leisure with a highlighter pen to hand. Mark any links you want to visit and add them to your favourites file or links bar offline, ready for when you next connect.

- **Compose all your e-mail messages offline** You can store messages in an out-tray with most mail software. No matter how many messages and how diverse their destinations, they will all be sent as part of the same phone call. Use the address book facility to store frequently used addresses.

- **Copy and paste e-mail for Web-based accounts** If you are using a Web-based e-mail account and cannot compose offline, write your message using a word processing package and copy it to the clipboard. Then go online, access your e-mail site and paste the message in.

- **Plan ahead** Have a clear idea of what you hope to get from a session on the Internet before you connect. Have e-mails ready to send and sites you want to visit on your links bar. If you know that you're likely to get carried away, set a timer to jolt you out of your absorption.

- **Keep an eye on downloads** When downloading software, check the size of the files and the time the transfer is likely to take. This will depend on your hardware, the various linking connections and the time of day. Once a program is downloading, it usually runs a clock to show you how long it will take; if that's too long, cancel it. If you decide to do a long download, don't go away and leave it. Keep checking that data is still coming through and that the clock is counting down. If something goes wrong, the data transfer can stop, but you are still paying for the telephone connection.

- **Only use the Internet when it's appropriate** Don't assume that the Internet is the best way to research everything. Some pages are only a reproduction of what is available, sometimes for free, in printed form or as a computer program.

- **Give up when you're losing** Telephones and computers are both wonderful tools when they work properly, and sources of immense frustration when they don't. Their complexity means that there will inevitably be times when things go wrong. If things aren't working properly, it's a good idea to take a break. It may be fixed by the time you come back.

SITES WORTH SEEING

Free Internet service providers

Freeserve

http://www.freeserve.net

Offers unlimited Internet access, e-mail and newsgroup facilities for free. Installation software can be picked up from any store in the Dixons retail group. Requires Windows 95 or later versions.

Aardvaak

http://www.aardvaak.co.uk

Arsenal Football Club

http://www.arsenal.co.uk

Cable and Wireless Internet

http://www.cwcom.net

Tesco

http://www.tesco.net

Virgin

http://www.virgin.net

The above are a selection from a growing number of free providers. They all want to attract new users to their free service and all offer something different. Compare them using information from their sites.

Accessibility

Bobby

http://www.cast.org/bobby

Web-based service that analyses the accessibility of Web pages for people with disabilities. Send the URL of a page and you get a full report on whether or not it meets the standard needed to display the Bobby icon. There are lots of links to information about computing accessibility issues.

Appendix

Microsoft's accessibility and disabilities site

`http://microsoft.com/enable`

Information and utilities to download that customize earlier versions of Windows (see Figure A.13).

What are Disabilities?

Individuals are not disabled. Rather, people have difficulties performing certain tasks, such as using a keyboard in a certain way. These difficulties are referred to as 'disabilities'. Disabilities can be divided into four general categories. These categories describe groups of disabilities covering a broad range of people with widely different levels of needs.

- **Visual Impairments**. Ranges from slightly reduced visual acuity to total blindness. Those with reduced visual acuity may only need images on a computer screen to be reasonably sized or specially enlarged, whilse users with more severe impairments may require output to be translated into spoken text or Braille.
- **Hearing Impairments**. Some individuals do not notice beeps or recognize spoken words. These users may require a program to prompt them in a different manner, such as a screen flash or displaying spoken messages as text.
- **Movement Impairments**. Some users may be unable to perform certain manual tasks. These can range from difficulty holding a book to the inability to type two keys at the same time. Other individuals may have a tendency to hit multiple keys, 'bounce' keys when pressing or releasing them, or be unable to manipulate a mouse. These individuals may require keyboards and mouse functions to be adapted to their requirements.
- **Cognitive and Language Impairments**. Cognitive impairments take many forms, including Downs Syndrome, short- and long-term memory impairments, and perceptual differences. Proper software design can help increase the number of people with mild cognitive impairments who can use computers. Language disorders include dyslexia, which can make reading or writing difficult. People attempting to learn new lanaguages also have temporary language impairments.
- **Seizure Disorders**. Specific patterns of light or sound can trigger epileptic seizures in some susceptible individuals.
- **Speech Impairments**. Physical impairments make speaking difficult for some individuals.

Figure A.13   Microsoft offers practical help for all users

Trace Research and Development Centre

`http://trace.wisc.edu`

The Centre publishes a database of computer products and provides related information for people with disabilities.

Web Accessibility Initiative (WAI)

`http://www.w3.org/WAI/References`

The WAI works to ensure that Internet technology is accessible to all and provides help for users and designers.

Other software

Unmozify

`http://www.evolve.co.uk`

Visit this site to read about and download this useful offline browsing software.

`http://tucows.cableinet.net`
`http://www.download.com`

Both are sites where you can search for and download software. Make sure you have an up-to-date virus checker or download one from here.

Free e-mail

Two providers

`http://www.hotmail.com`
`http://www.bigfoot.com`

Mail forwarders

A selection of providers

`http://www.iname.com`
`http://www.netforward.com`
`http://www.myownemail.com`

All have large selections of interesting aliases that are yours to keep forever. You can have lots of fun creating a new identity!

sites worth seeing

Directories of mailing lists

Mailbase

http://www.mailbase.ac.uk

Look here for a directory of all UK academic mailing lists (see Figure A.10). The site includes tutorials on how to use Mailbase.

Other sites to try

http://www.liszt.com

http://www.neosoft.com/internet/paml

Both these sites will find, categorize, describe and give details of how to subscribe to lists.

Directories of newsgroups

Note: Apart from the addresses given below, newsgroup postings can be also searched for on AltaVista, Hot Bot, Excite and Yahoo!.

DejaNews

http://www.dejanews.com

This is a searchable archive of postings to newsgroups. It is good for reading old articles and getting a feel for what different groups are about.

Kovacs

http://www.mailbase.ac.uk/kovacs

Most academic newsgroups and related resources can be found here.

Finding e-mail addresses

People Search

http://www.w3com.com/psearch

Sends to four address searchers at once. Efficient way of finding elusive addresses.

Browser software

Netscape Navigator and Microsoft Internet Explorer

http://www.netscape.com
http://www.microsoft.com/ie

Downloads, upgrades, anything you might ever want to do with a browser can be done on these sites.

Academic and general search tools

Note: If you want to know more about searching the Web or wish to access tutorials on it, look at:

http://www.searchenginewatch.com

You can register for a free e-mail newsletter to keep you up to date with search tool developments.

The Academic Directory

http://acdc.hensa.ac.uk

This is an effective tool for searching the UK academic Internet (see Figure A.8).

AltaVista

http://www.altavista.com

Search engine with lots of interesting features, including a facility to translate Web pages or your own text from English to French, German, Spanish, Italian or Portuguese and vice versa at amazing speeds. It is not always idiomatic, but, nevertheless, needs to be seen to be believed.

BUBL

http://www.bubl.ac.uk

This site acts as an information service for the UK academic community. There are links from here to sites dealing with all subjects, journals, mailing lists and much more (see Figure 1.4).

Dogpile

http://www.dogpile.com

A multi-engine search tool that 'fetches' links for you to look at. It searches Web sites and newsgroups. You can even arrange the order in which the 20+ engines and directories it searches are visited. Use it to look at how different engines respond to the same search.

Excite Search

http://www.excite.com

One of the biggest of the search engines. It also offers free e-mail.

HotBot

http://www.hotbot.com

Powerful search engine of similar size to Excite. It claims to update daily and search results show the date written.

Internet Magazine

http://internet-magazine.com

One of the many publications that deal with this subject. This magazine's Web site lists, evaluates and links to all the major UK ISPs and gives details of their charges (see Figure A.14). It also has a list of all UK cybercafés.

Yahoo!

http://www.yahoo.com
http://www.yahoo.co.uk

The second address is for British sites. This search directory has well-organized sections on a wide range of topics. It gives access to text-based information, chat sessions and message boards.

full UK coverage

ISP home   submit ISP details   home

Company	Tel No		Cost	Backbone
AAP Internet	(0181) 427 1166	Email	£10.99	Netkonect
Aardvaak Connect Free	na	Email	Free	Not Known
X Stream	(0870) 730 6466	Email	Free	Colt Internet
Zetnet Services	(01595) 696 667	Email	£7.50*	BTnet / Wisper
Zoo Internet	(0345) 326 326	Email	£6.99	Zoo Internet
Zulu Internet	(01494) 758 895	Email	£10	Nildram
Zynet	(01392) 209 500	Email	£10	GX Networks

mailto:info@aardvaak.co.uk

Figure A.14 *Internet Magazine* carries an A–Z of providers with links to their e-mail, making it easy to request details

sites worth seeing

Glossary

Bit Short for 'binary digit', it is the smallest unit of information stored on a computer. The speed at which a modem transfers data is measured in bits per second (bps).

Bookmark A stored URL that gives you subsequent access to that site with a single click of the mouse. Other names for this include hot list and favourite place.

Browser Software that enables you to view documents on the World Wide Web.

Cache The cache stores the information downloaded from the Internet on your computer. This enables you to reload quickly on subsequent visits and to look at pages offline.

Cybercafé A café with computers where you can eat, drink and access the Internet. A growing phenomenon.

Download Transfer of information from a computer on the Internet to your own computer.

e-mail Short for 'electronic mail'. A system for sending messages and files from one Internet-linked computer to another.

Encryption Writing messages in coded form to ensure they can only be read by recipients who have the key to that code.

FAQ The letters stand for 'frequently asked questions'. Web sites and newsgroups have lists of these to help you make good use of what they offer (and to prevent you being a nuisance by asking something that's already been asked thousands of times).

Freeware Software that is completely free.

FTP The letters stand for 'file transfer protocol'. This is a method of transferring files from one computer to another.

Gateway sites These act as signposts. They contain links to large numbers of other sites on a particular topic.

Hard disk The disk that is part of your computer. This is where most of the information on the computer is stored. Floppy disks are smaller versions of this and can be used to copy and moves files between computers.

HTML This stands for 'hyper text mark-up language'. This is the computer language in which Web pages are written. You don't need to understand it unless you want to write Web pages of your own. To see what it looks like, go to 'view document source' for any Web page.

Hypertext link An image or piece of text on a Web page that provides a link to another site or document.

Internet A worldwide network of linked computers.

Internet relay chat (IRC) A 'live' discussion on the Internet where users talk by typing messages to each other.

Internet service provider (ISP) An organization that provides you with Internet access.

Intranet A mini Internet within an organization. Most universities and schools have an intranet on their network of computers. This can be kept private or made accessible to general Web users.

Modem The device that connects your computer to the phone network.

Netiquette Internet etiquette. A loose set of 'rules' about how to behave when using the Internet, which particularly applies to newsgroups.

Newsgroup An Internet discussion group. There are groups for every topic imaginable.

Offline browser Software that allows you to view previously accessed Web pages and links without connecting to the Internet.

Online When you are connected to the Internet via the phone network.

Plug-ins A piece of software that allows your computer to perform extra functions. Sometimes these are necessary to view a Web page properly. Most pages that require a plug-in offer links to free downloads.

Point of presence (POP)   The phone number that connects you to your ISP.

Search engine/directory   A facility that acts as an index to the Internet and allows you to search for relevant documents.

Secure sockets layer (SSL)   Internet security system that encodes the data you send so no one can read or change it during transmission. Financial transactions and the transfer of other sensitive data should be done only through secure sites.

Shareware   Software that can be tried out for free for a limited period. Continued use requires a fee to be paid to the author.

Uniform resource locator (URL)   The address of a web site. Every Web page has a unique URL.

Virus   A virus is designed to disrupt the working of a computer. Viruses can be transferred from one computer to another. It is essential to install software that checks for viruses before you download anything from the Web. If you have a virus, it can also be 'cleaned up' by this software.

Web page   A document viewed on the Web. It can be several paper pages long.

Web site   A collection of Web pages.

World Wide Web   The most widely used part of the Internet. It allows publication of, and access to, documents. Also referred to as WWW, W3 and the Web.

Index

Index

Visit Kogan Page on-line

Comprehensive information on
Kogan Page titles

Features include

- complete catalogue listings,
  including book reviews and
  descriptions

- special monthly promotions

- information on NEW titles and
  BESTSELLING titles

- a secure shopping basket facility
  for on-line ordering

PLUS everything you need to know
about KOGAN PAGE

http://www.kogan-page.co.uk